MW00885512

Grandma's
A Little Bit
of Everything
Cookbook

Dedication

This book is dedicated to my Mother and Grandmother, who believe in me.

This book is also dedicated to those friends that my grandmother loved so well to play golf, cards and all around have fun. She said,"Always live your life day by day", and she did. I remember having fun with her on many occasions at the golf course, with her friends, and the potlucks they would spend the morning making and the afternoon eating. Some of these recipes are from them. They all had something yummy cooking in their kitchens. So I wish to dedicate this book to them.

Mari Gernandt (My Nama)
Judy Hazelwood
Betty Mcallister
Char Wendell
Arlone Gifford
Fran Osgood (Aunt Fran)
Ruthie Wetterstrom
Rene Gruthoff
Gerri Hoban (The Tomato)
Irene Sheppard
Marrion Cross

I want you all to know I have never forgotten you! Love always!

Grandma's
A Little Bit of Everything
Cookbook

Featuring over 200 easy everyday ingredients recipes. Converted from my Grandmother's kitchen. Additional recipe information with nutritional values and substitute values for cooking fat free.

Editorial Credits
Victoria Clasper
Cover Artist Holly Whitten
(My Dear Mom)

Copyright©2008

Table of Contents

Appetizers and Beverages

APPETIZERS AND BEVERAGES

Crab or Clam Dip

Soften together over low heat and add one can minced clams with juice, or 1 can of crab meat. Set the juice aside. You can also use fresh crab meat.. Mix all ingredients together. If you need it spicy then add more Tabasco if less add less Tabasco. If to thick, thin with the clam or crab juice. This will keep 4 top 5 days in the refrigerator.

Serving 4-6
Yield: 2 1/2 cups
Start to finish: 10 minutes

16 ounces cream cheese
1/2 stick butter or margarine
1 tablespoon Worcestershire sauce
3 dashes Tabasco sauce
6 1/2 ounces clams
Several dashes of hot sauce
or Tabasco sauce (more to taste)

Nutritional Values:
Per Serving: 356 Calories; 34g Fat (85.6% calories from fat); 10g Protein; 3g Carbohydrate; 0g Dietary Fiber; 114mg Cholesterol; 345mg Sodium.
Points: 10

Substitute Values:
Per Serving (using fat-free substitutes): 164 Calories; 9g Fat (49.0% calories from fat); 15g Protein; 6g Carbohydrate; 0g Dietary Fiber; 16mg Cholesterol; 641mg Sodium.
Points: 3

Herbed Yogurt Seafood Dip

An excellent party dip to serve with chilled cooked shrimp, crab legs, cubes of cooked lobster, raw oysters and or clams.
Combine all the ingredients except the paprika and chill. Serve garnished with paprika and surrounded with the seafood.

Servings: 4-6
Yield: 2 1/2 cups
Start to finish: 20 minutes

1 cup mayonnaise
1 cup yogurt
1/2 cup green onions, chopped with tops
1 tablespoon lemon juice
1/8 cup fresh parsley
1/8 cup tarragon
1/8 cup basil
1/8 cup dill
dash salt
dash pepper
Garnish with Paprika

Nutritional Values:
Per Serving : 322 Calories; 35g Fat (91.2% calories from fat); 3g Protein; 5g Carbohydrate; 1g Dietary Fiber; 21mg Cholesterol; 284mg Sodium.
Points: 9

Substitute Values:
Per Serving (using fat-free substitutes): 87 Calories; 2g Fat (24.3% calories from fat); 3g Protein; 14g Carbohydrate; 1g Dietary Fiber; 3mg Cholesterol; 592mg Sodium.
Points: 2

Walking Taco

Arrange on a plate refried beans first and then avocado. Then layer rest of ingredients and be creative. Scoop with your favorite tortilla chips or Frito's.

Servings: 4
Yield: 3 Cups
Start to finish: 20 minutes

16 ounces refried beans, canned
2 whole avocado, mashed
2 medium fresh tomato, chopped
2 whole green onion, chopped
4 ounces Ortega chili, chopped
4 ounces olive, chopped
1 cup cheddar cheese, shredded

Nutritional Values:
Per Serving : 477 Calories; 31g Fat (55.3% calories from fat); 19g Protein; 37g Carbohydrate; 12g Dietary Fiber; 35mg Cholesterol; 1069mg Sodium.
Points: 11

Substitute Values:
Per Serving (using fat-free substitutes): 403 Calories; 21g Fat (45.1% calories from fat); 21g Protein; 38g Carbohydrate; 12g Dietary Fiber; 10mg Cholesterol; 1096mg Sodium.
Points: 10

Crab Appetizer

Heat soup on low until smooth. Add gelatin that has been mixed with the 3 tablespoons water. Stir and let cool. Add to remaining ingredients. Add crab last. Pour into mold. Let stand overnight in refrigerator.

Servings: 1
Yield: 2-3 cups
Start to finish: 20 minutes preparation and overnight setting.

4 1/4 ounces black olives, chopped
1 cup mayonnaise
8 ounces cream cheese
1/2 cup celery, finely chopped
1 can mushroom soup, no water added
1 package Knox gelatin
3 tablespoons water
6 ounces crab meat, canned
salt, to taste
pepper, to taste

Nutritional Values:
Per Serving: 469 Calories; 48g Fat (88.7% calories from fat); 10g Protein; 4g Carbohydrate; 1g Dietary Fiber; 80mg Cholesterol; 745mg Sodium.
Points: 13

Substitute Values:
Per Serving (using fat-free substitutes): 143 Calories; 4g Fat (28.6% calories from fat); 12g Protein; 13g Carbohydrate; 1g Dietary Fiber; 29mg Cholesterol; 1138mg Sodium.
Points: 3

Crab Mold

Mix gelatin in water and add to heated soup. Mix cheese and Miracle Whip® until smooth. Add celery onion and crab. Mix all ingredients together and pour into greased mold. Refrigerate overnight. Un-mold and place on plate lined with red lettuce. Serve with crackers or for spread on fresh vegetables.

Servings: 1
Yield: 3 cups

1 can cream of mushroom soup
3 ounces cream cheese
1 envelope gelatin
4 tablespoons water
1 cup Miracle Whip®
1 cup celery
1 small onion
6 1/2 ounces crab meat, canned or fresh

Nutritional Values:
Per Serving: 388 Calories; 38g Fat (84.1% calories from fat); 9g Protein; 7g Carbohydrate; 1g Dietary Fiber; 56mg Cholesterol; 552mg Sodium.
Points: 11

Substitute Values:
Per Serving (using fat-free substitutes): 121 Calories; 2g Fat (15.9% calories from fat); 9g Protein; 16g Carbohydrate; 1g Dietary Fiber; 29mg Cholesterol; 886mg Sodium.
Points: 2

Hot Crab Meat Yogurt Canapés

Combine crab meat, cheese and mustard. Fold in the yogurt, enough to bind the mixture. Season with cayenne, salt and pepper. Spoon the crab meat mixture onto the rounds of bread. Put under the broiler about 3 in. from heat for 2-3 min. Decorate each one with parsley or paprika.

Servings: 4
Yield: 25 pieces
Start to finish: 10 minutes

2 cup crab meat, cleaned, flaked
1/2 cup parmesan cheese
1 teaspoon prepared mustard
1/2 cup plain yogurt
dash cayenne
salt, to taste
pepper, to taste
fresh parsley or paprika as a garnish
25 small rounds bread (white or dark)

Nutritional Values:
Per Serving: 132 Calories; 5g Fat (34.4% calories from fat); 19g Protein; 2g Carbohydrate; trace Dietary Fiber; 72mg Cholesterol; 441mg Sodium's.
Points: 3

Substitute Values:
Per Serving (using fat-free substitutes):121 Calories; 1g Fat (7.1% calories from fat); 20g Protein; 7g Carbohydrate; trace Dietary Fiber; 73mg Cholesterol; 372mg Sodium.
Points: 3

Zucchini Appetizer

Stir together eggs and oil, and Bis quick Then add the remainder of ingredients. Add zucchini last. Bake qt 350° for 35 min. or until nicely browned. Cut into small squares and serve hot.

Servings: 4
Yield: 3 cups
Start to finish: 45 minutes

3 cups zucchini, sliced thin
1 cup Bisquick® baking mix
1/2 cup onion
1/2 cup parmesan cheese
4 eggs, beaten
1/2 teaspoon seasoned salt
1/2 teaspoon marjoram
dash pepper
1 clove garlic
1/2 cup vegetable oil

Nutritional Values:
Per Serving: 503 Calories; 39g Fat (69.8% calories from fat); 14g Protein; 25g Carbohydrate; 2g Dietary Fiber; 220mg Cholesterol; 781mg Sodium.
Points: 13

Substitute Values:
Per Serving: (using substitute Enova cooking oil, fat-free Parmesan cheese and egg substitute) 230 Calories; 4g Fat (17.1% calories from fat); 18g Protein; 30g Carbohydrate; 2g Dietary Fiber; 12mg Cholesterol; 802mg Sodium.
Points: 5

Cheese Puffs

Cut crusts from bread and cut in cubes about size of a marshmallow. Melt cheese and butter. Whip eggs until stiff and add cheese mixture. Dip cubes in mixture and put on cookie sheet. Cover and refrigerate 24 hours. Bake at 400 degrees for 5-8 min. until golden.

Serving Ideas: Make 1 ½ recipe to cover cubes from whole loaf. After refrigerating them, place on cookie sheet and place in freezer or place into plastic bag and use as needed.

1 loaf French bread, cut in 1" cubes
3 ounces cream cheese
2 pads margarine
3/4 cup cheddar cheese
3 egg whites

Nutritional Values:
Per Serving (excluding unknown items): 593 Calories; 42g Fat (63.9% calories from fat); 13g Protein; 40g Carbohydrate; 2g Dietary Fiber; 30mg Cholesterol; 973mg Sodium.
Points: 15

Substitute Values:
Per Serving: (using fat-free substitutes): 266 Calories; 4g Fat (14.9% calories from fat); 15g Protein; 41g Carbohydrate; 2g Dietary Fiber; 4mg Cholesterol; 713mg Sodium.
Points: 5

Chicken and Ham Pin-wheels

Flatten breasts with a mallet. Sprinkle mixed seasoning's on breasts. Place ham slices on top and roll. Secure with toothpicks. Place seam down in baking pan. Pour lemon juice over. Bake at 350 degrees for about 20 min. Cool and refrigerate. Slice in ½ inch thick slices and serve.

Servings: 4
Yield: 10 pinwheels

2 chicken breast, no skin, no bone, flattened
6 ham slice, thinly sliced
1/8 teaspoon dried basil
1/8 teaspoon salt
dash garlic salt
1/2 cup lemon juice

Nutritional Values:
Per Serving: 219 Calories; 8g Fat (35.7% calories from fat); 32g Protein; 3g Carbohydrate; trace Dietary Fiber; 88mg Cholesterol; 561mg Sodium.
Points: 5

Substitute Values:
Per Serving: (using lean meat substitutes) 184 Calories; 3g Fat (15.9% calories from fat); 34g Protein; 3g Carbohydrate; trace Dietary Fiber; 94mg Cholesterol; 699mg Sodium.
Points: 4

Chicken Liver Pate'

Render chicken fat with slices of one onion. Strain fat into jar (no onion). Put livers in a pan and bake at 350° until done. Chop 1 onion into fine pieces – also chop eggs and livers very fine and mix together. Keep adding about 2 Tablespoons chicken fat to mixture until texture is like pate' (smooth). Add salt to taste.

Servings: 6
Yield: 2 cups

Notes: Keep refrigerated (keeps only 2 days) but bring to room temperature before serving with crackers.

1/2 pound chicken liver
2 egg, hard-boiled
2 medium onion
1 small package Chicken Fat

Nutritional Values:
Per Serving: 395 Calories; 37g Fat (85.8% calories from fat); 9g Protein; 5g Carbohydrate; 1g Dietary Fiber; 266mg Cholesterol; 52mg Sodium.
Points: 11

Substitute Values:
Per Serving: (using fat-free substitutes, margarine instead of chicken fat) 154 Calories; 11g Fat (63.2% calories from fat); 9g Protein; 5g Carbohydrate; 1g Dietary Fiber; 237mg Cholesterol; 237mg Sodium.
Points: 4

Spanish Bread

This spread you can make a head of time, freeze if you want, or refrigerate. Combine all ingredients. Spread on French rolls or French bread halves. Put under the broiler until cheese bubbles watch closely. About 1 to 2 min.

Servings: 6
Yield: 4 cups
Start to finish: 30 minutes

1 pound Cheddar Cheese, shredded
1 can ripe olive
1 can chilies
1 can tomato sauce
2 medium onions, finely chopped
2 cloves garlic, minced
3 tablespoons vinegar
Tabasco sauce, to taste
salt and pepper, to taste
French rolls (6 rolls per pkg.)

Nutritional Values:
Per Serving: 337 Calories; 25g Fat (66.5% calories from fat); 20g Protein; 9g Carbohydrate; 1g Dietary Fiber; 79mg Cholesterol; 725mg Sodium.
Points: 9

Substitute Values:
Per Serving (using fat-free cheddar): 141 Calories; trace Fat (1.4% calories from fat); 25g Protein; 10g Carbohydrate; 1g Dietary Fiber; 14mg Cholesterol; 796mg Sodium.
Points: 3

Pizza Bread

Mix together and spread on small slices of bread and bake 20 min. at 350 degrees.

Servings: 4
Start to finish: 30 minutes

Serving Ideas: 1 Loaf Sour Dough bread recommended.

1 cup tomato paste
1/2 cup vegetable oil
1 small onion, chopped
1 clove garlic
dash oregano
1/2 cup ripe olive, chopped
1 1/2 cups cheddar cheese, grated

Nutritional Values:
Per Serving: 497 Calories; 44g Fat (76.4% calories from fat); 13g Protein; 17g Carbohydrate; 4g Dietary Fiber; 45mg Cholesterol; 930mg Sodium.
Points: 14

Substitute Values:
Per Serving (using fat-free substitutes and Canola oil): 386 Calories; 29g Fat (65.9% calories from fat); 16g Protein; 18g Carbohydrate; 4g Dietary Fiber; 8mg Cholesterol; 970mg Sodium.
Points: 9

Shrimp Cocktail Brasilienne Supreme

Combine dressing mixture. Cover bottom of cocktail cup with pineapple tid-bits. Add shrimp, dressing, and top with almonds and cherry.

Servings: 10
Yield: 4 cocktail cups
Start to finish: 20 minutes

Dressing:
3 cups mayonnaise
3/4 cup honey
1/2 teaspoon salt
3 tablespoons fresh ginger
1/4 cup cider vinegar
1 tablespoon white pepper
1/2 cup orange juice

Nutritional Values:
Per Serving (excluding unknown items): 572 Calories; 56g Fat (82.6% calories from fat); 3g Protein; 23g Carbohydrate; trace Dietary Fiber; 40mg Cholesterol; 500mg Sodium.
Points: 16

Substitute Values:
Per Serving (using substitute fat-free mayonnaise, sugar substitutes, and egg substitute): 157 Calories; trace Fat (1.3% calories from fat); 3g Protein; 38g Carbohydrate; trace Dietary Fiber; 17mg Cholesterol; 1037mg Sodium.
Points: 3

Blackberry Farm Punch

This drink is so yummy. Every time I make this I get raves and asked about the recipe. Mix all together and chill. Pour over ice. Watch out this has a bite!

Servings: 24
Yield: 24 servings

16 ounces cranberry juice cocktail
46 fluid ounces pineapple juice
4 liters ginger ale, (2 bottles)
(for adults only add:)
1 Fifth of vodka

Nutritional Values:
Per Serving: 245 Calories; trace Fat (0.8% calories from fat); trace Protein; 18g Carbohydrate; trace Dietary Fiber; 0mg Cholesterol; 8mg Sodium.
Points: 5

Substitute Values:
Per Serving (using fat-free substitutes): Not much to substitute here...:)
Points: 5

Bloody Mary Mix

In a tall glass add all ingredients.

4 dashes Worcestershire sauce
2 dashes Angastora bitters
2 drops Tabasco sauce
3 dashes celery salt
3 dashes salt
2 dashes pepper
1/2 ounce sweet and sour lemon mix
or whiskey sour mix
1 1/4 ounces vodka

Nutritional Values:
Per Serving : 88 Calories; trace Fat (23.1% calories from fat); trace Protein; 1g Carbohydrate; trace Dietary Fiber; 0mg Cholesterol; 1419mg Sodium.
Points: 2

Homemade Kalau'ha

Combine and add 1 fifth Vodka. Pour into gallon jug and add vanilla bean. Let stand 3-4 weeks.

(much cheaper than the real thing and taste just like it).

2 oz. Jar Espresso instant coffee
2 Cups boiling water
4 cups sugar
1 fifth vodka
vanilla bean

Nutritional Values:
Per Serving: 591 Calories; 0g Fat (0.0% calories from fat); 0g Protein; 100g Carbohydrate; 0g Dietary Fiber; 0mg Cholesterol; 4mg Sodium.
Points: 12

Homemade Beer

Mix and let stand with cloth over it until it sets on the "red" line of beer tester.

Servings: 150
Yield: 10 gallons

10 gallons water
2 quarts malt
2 tablespoons salt
10 pounds sugar
2 yeast cake

Nutritional Values:
Per Serving: 117 Calories; trace Fat (0.0% calories from fat); trace Protein; 30g Carbohydrate; trace Dietary Fiber; 0mg Cholesterol; 93mg Sodium.
Points: 2

Soups and Salads

SOUPS AND SALADS

Onion Soup

Cook onions in butter and oil, slowly and covered for 15min. Uncover and sprinkle on salt and sugar. Raise heat and cook 30 minutes. Add: 1 or 2 Tablespoons flour and 3 ¼ pints boiling bouillon. Then add dry white wine or vermouth. Salt and pepper to taste. Garnish each serving with croûtons and Parmesan cheese.

Servings: 6
Yield: 6
Start to finish: 30 minutes

1 1/2 pounds onions, thinly sliced
1 1/2 ounces butter
1 tablespoon vegetable oil
1 teaspoon salt
1/2 tablespoon sugar
2 tablespoons flour
3 1/4 pints boiling bouillon
1/2 pint dry white wine or vermouth
salt and pepper to taste
1 cup croûtons
1 cup Parmesan cheese

Nutritional Values:
Per Serving: 184 Calories; 12g Fat (58.7% calories from fat); 7g Protein; 12g Carbohydrate; 2g Dietary Fiber; 26mg Cholesterol; 665mg Sodium.
Points: 12

Substitute Values:
Per Serving (using fat-free substitutes): 145 Calories; 5g Fat (30.8% calories from fat); 8g Protein; 18g Carbohydrate; 2g Dietary Fiber; 16mg Cholesterol; 570mg Sodium.
Points: 3

Very fresh Tomato Soup

Simmer the above ingredients for 30 min. puree and strain. Mix together 3 T cornstarch and 3 T butter melted. Stir into soup to thicken, over medium heat. Add 2 T brown sugar 2 tsp salt and pepper to taste. Then stir into the very hot soup 2 C light cream and 1 egg yolk beaten. Simmer additional 15 min.

Servings: 6
Start to finish: 1 hour

12 tomato, peeled and cubed, very ripe
1 cup celery, sliced
1/4 cup parsley, minced
1 cup chicken stock
1/2 cup onion, sliced
3 tablespoons cornstarch
3 tablespoons butter, melted
2 tablespoons brown sugar
2 teaspoons salt and pepper, to taste
2 cups light cream
1 egg yolk, beaten

Nutritional Values:
Per Serving: 309 Calories; 23g Fat (64.3% calories from fat); 5g Protein; 23g Carbohydrate; 3g Dietary Fiber; 104mg Cholesterol; 966mg Sodium.
Points: 7

Substitute Values:
Per Serving (using imitation margarine, splenda brown sugar and evaporated skim milk): 180 Calories; 4g Fat (24.7% calories from fat); 9g Protein; 21g Carbohydrate; 2g Dietary Fiber; 39mg Cholesterol; 1031mg Sodium.
Points: 4

Gazpacho

Combine all ingredients except cucumber. Let stand at room temp for 1 hour, stirring often. Chill for at least 2 hours. Add cucumber just before serving.

Servings: 6
Yield: 5 cups
Start to finish: 2 hours 10 minutes

4 cups tomato, peeled and chopped
1/2 cup green pepper, chopped
3/4 cup onion, chopped
1 clove garlic, minced
2 cups beef bouillon
1/2 cup lemon juice
1 tablespoon canola oil
1/2 cup cucumber, diced
1 tablespoon salt
pepper, fresh ground

Nutritional Values:
Per Serving: 70 Calories; 3g Fat (34.2% calories from fat); 2g Protein; 11g Carbohydrate; 2g Dietary Fiber; 0mg Cholesterol; 1532mg Sodium.
Points: 1

Avocado Molded Salad

Dissolve the Jello in boiling water. Add cold water and seasoning's. Chill till almost set. Fold in cottage cheese, olives and mashed avocados. Chill until set..

Servings: 4
Start to finish: 2 hours

6 ounces lime jello
2 cups water, boiling
1 1/2 cups water, cold
1/4 teaspoon salt and pepper
2 tablespoons vinegar
1 tablespoon onion, grated
1 pint cottage cheese
3 ounces green olive, sliced thin
2 avocado, ripe

Nutritional Values:
Per Serving: 290 Calories; 20g Fat (58.8% calories from fat); 18g Protein; 14g Carbohydrate; 3g Dietary Fiber; 9mg Cholesterol; 749mg Sodium.
Points: 8

Substitute Values:
Per Serving (using fat-free cottage cheese. And jell-o sugar free fat free substitutes): 258 Calories; 18g Fat (57.5% calories from fat); 17g Protein; 12g Carbohydrate; 3g Dietary Fiber; 5mg Cholesterol; 590mg Sodium.
Points: 6

Crabby Ol' Aspic

Combine first 6 ingredients. Simmer uncovered 10min. Strain. Mix quickly with jello, then add remaining tomato juice and vinegar. Chill mixture until consistency of unbeaten egg whites. Fold in crab and chopped celery. Line bottom of mold with sliced olives. Pour mixture in pan, chill until firm. Un-mold on greens. Serve with mayonnaise, if desired.

Servings: 8
Preparation Time: 25 minutes
Start to finish: 2 hours

Notes: You may also use shrimp, tune or slivered ham.

3 cups tomato juice, canned
1 stalk celery
1 small onion
1 bay leaf
1 teaspoon Salt
1/8 teaspoon Pepper
1 package lemon jello, large
2/3 cup tomato juice, cold
1/4 cup vinegar
1 cup Spanish olives, sliced
1 cup crab or fresh crab, canned
1/4 cup celery, chopped

Nutritional Values:
Per Serving (excluding unknown items): 389 Calories; 25g Fat (56.7% calories from fat); 24g Protein; 18g Carbohydrate; 3g Dietary Fiber; 271mg Cholesterol; 847mg Sodium. Exchanges: 1/2 Grain(Starch); 3 Lean Meat; 1 1/2 Vegetable; 3 Fat.
Points: 9

Substitute Values:
Per Serving (using fat-free substitutes):242 Calories; 6g Fat (21.6% calories from fat); 28g Protein; 20g Carbohydrate; 3g Dietary Fiber; 222mg Cholesterol; 900mg Sodium.
Points: 5

Lime Jello Salad

Dissolve gelatin in hot water. Cool. Mash cream cheese and add pineapple, celery and nuts. Fold into gelatin. Chill until thickened. Fold in whipped cream. Pour into mold and chill until firm.

Servings: 8
Start to finish: 2 hours

2 packages lime jello, small
2 cups water, hot
6 ounces cream cheese
1 small pineapple, crushed
1 cup celery, diced
1 cup pecan, chopped
1/2 pint light cream, whipped

Nutritional Values:
Per Serving (excluding unknown items): 298 Calories; 28g Fat (80.3% calories from fat); 4g Protein; 12g Carbohydrate; 2g Dietary Fiber; 64mg Cholesterol; 90mg Sodium.
Points: 8

Substitute Values:
Per Serving (using fat-free substitutes): 200 Calories; 15g Fat (66.1% calories from fat); 5g Protein; 13g Carbohydrate; 2g Dietary Fiber; 22mg Cholesterol; 143mg Sodium.
Points: 5

New Zealand Fruit Salad Pavlova

Prepare a baking tray by lining with foil and greasing with melted butter.
Beat the egg whites and salt until soft peaks form when the beater is lifter from the mixture. Add the sugar, a little at a time, beating we after each addition. Continue to beat until the mixture is very stiff. Add cornstarch, vinegar and vanilla. Beat thoroughly.

Pile mixture into a circle about 10 inches round on a prepared baking tray. Bake at 250 degrees for 1 ½ hours. Turn oven off and leave the Pavlova in oven with door closed until completely cold. Remove carefully from foil and place Pavlova on serving plate. Just before serving whip cream until stiff. Spread over the Pavlova. Prepare fruit and arrange on cream.

Seasonal New Zealand fruits to offer guests include passion fruit pulp, sliced kiwi fruit, feijoas and tamarillos.

Servings: 6

Notes: Seasonal New Zealand fruits to offer guests include passion fruit pulp, sliced kiwi fruit, feijoas, tamarillos.

4 egg whites
1/4 teaspoon salt
1 cup sugar granulated
4 teaspoons cornstarch
2 teaspoons vinegar
1/2 teaspoon vanilla
1 cup cream
2 cups fruit

Nutritional Values:
Per Serving (excluding unknown items): 245 Calories; 10g Fat (35.9% calories from fat); 3g Protein; 37g Carbohydrate; trace Dietary Fiber; 35mg Cholesterol; 141mg Sodium.
Points: 13

Substitute Values:
Per Serving (using fat-free substitutes: evaporated skim milk and a sugar substitutes):116 Calories; trace Fat (0.7% calories from fat); 6g Protein; 21g Carbohydrate; trace Dietary Fiber; 2mg Cholesterol; 239mg Sodium.
Points: 2

Red Snapper Salad

(This is the poor man's substitute for Crab Louie.)

Broil fish 7 min. on each side and let cool, then prepare as any salad. Break up fish in bite sizes. Use Italian dressing with a few dollops of miracle whip on the fish. Make the salads in 2 big bowls.

Serves: 2

2 Filet's of red snapper cooked
head of iceberg lettuce
2 tomatoes
raw zucchini or cauliflower if desired

Nutritional Values:
Per Serving (excluding unknown items): 137 Calories; 2g Fat (11.4% calories from fat); 21g Protein; 11g Carbohydrate; 4g Dietary Fiber; 31mg Cholesterol; 85mg Sodium.
Points: 2

Heavenly Chicken Salad

Place chicken, celery, mushrooms, pecans and bacon in a large mixing bowl. In separate bowl mix mayonnaise, sour cream , lemon juice and salt. Pour over the other ingredients and toss.

Servings: 4

4 cups diced cooked chicken
2 cups celery, diced
4 1/2 ounces mushroom
1/2 cup pecan, toasted and sliced
1 cup mayonnaise
1 cup sour cream
1 1/2 teaspoons salt
2 tablespoons lemon juice
4 bacon, slices, crumbled

Nutritional Values:
Per Serving (excluding unknown items): 663 Calories; 71g Fat (91.1% calories from fat); 7g Protein; 9g Carbohydrate; 2g Dietary Fiber; 50mg Cholesterol; 1297mg Sodium.
Points: 19

Substitute Values:
Per Serving (using fat-free mayonnaise and sour cream): 232 Calories; 12g Fat (45.5% calories from fat); 8g Protein; 25g Carbohydrate; 2g Dietary Fiber; 12mg Cholesterol; 1757mg Sodium.
Points: 5

Chicken Salad Oriental

Stir together the chicken, mayonnaise, mustard, celery, sprouts, green onion and sesame oil. Season to taste with salt and pepper. Cover and chill until serving.

To serve: Arrange 4 slices pineapple on chopped lettuce of spinach beds. Spoon chicken salad on to the pineapple slices, adding the chow mien noodles just before serving (to keep them crisp).

Serves 4

2 cups cooked chicken, or turkey diced
1/2 cup mayonnaise
1/2 cup Dijon mustard
1/2 cup celery, thinly sliced
1/4 cup green onion, chopped
pinch salt and pepper, to taste
1/2 teaspoon sesame oil
8 ounces pineapple, canned and drained (4slices)
1 1/2 cups bean sprouts
1 1/2 cups chow mien noodles

Nutritional Values:
Per Serving (excluding unknown items): 465 Calories; 34g Fat (62.9% calories from fat); 26g Protein; 19g Carbohydrate; 3g Dietary Fiber; 69mg Cholesterol; 677mg Sodium.
Points: 12

Substitute Values:
Per Serving (using fat-free mayonnaise): 292 Calories; 10g Fat (31.8% calories from fat); 26g Protein; 25g Carbohydrate; 3g Dietary Fiber; 60mg Cholesterol; 900mg Sodium.
Points: 6

Shrimp Mold

Heat tomato soup and bring to boil. Add cream cheese and stir until dissolve. Cool. Add celery,onion, mayonnaise and shrimp. Dissolve 1 ½ T gelatin in ¼ C boiling water. Pour into tomato soup mixture. Pour into lightly oiled mold. Let set overnight in refrigerator, or make early in am. May be served with cocktails on rye bread or as a dip (omitting gelatin).

Servings: 6
Start to finish: 20 minutes preparation and overnight setting.

2 cans shrimp, small
1 can tomato soup
12 ounces cream cheese
1 1/2 tablespoons gelatin, Knox
3/4 cup celery, finely chopped
1/2 cup onion, diced
1 cup mayonnaise

Nutritional Values:
Per Serving (excluding unknown items): 487 Calories; 51g Fat (90.4% calories from fat); 6g Protein; 7g Carbohydrate; 1g Dietary Fiber; 78mg Cholesterol; 510mg Sodium.
Points: 14

Substitute Values:
Per Serving (using tomato soup, reduced fat, condensed, fat-free cream cheese, and fat-free mayonnaise): 113 Calories; 1g Fat (8.7% calories from fat); 9g Protein; 17g Carbohydrate; 1g Dietary Fiber; 8mg Cholesterol; 909mg Sodium.
Points: 2

Shrimp in Pineapple Shells

Halve pineapples lengthwise – leaves intact. Scoop out fruit and chop. Peel, remove white membrane of oranges and cut in small pieces. Peel and slice avocados., brush with lemon juice. Mix shrimp and fruits in bowl, add favorite dressing. Heat prepared pineapple shells in oven at 250° for 10.

Servings: 4
Start to finish: 30 minutes

3 cups pineapples, (3 small and ripe)
3 cups oranges, chopped
1 1/2 avocado, sliced
4 tablespoons lemon juice
2 pounds shrimp, cooked, and shelled

Nutritional Values:
Per Serving (excluding unknown items): 470 Calories; 15g Fat (27.2% calories from fat); 51g Protein; 37g Carbohydrate; 7g Dietary Fiber; 443mg Cholesterol; 517mg Sodium.
Points: 10

Seven Layer Salad

Fill large bowl half full of shredded lettuce (packaged or half a head of lettuce shredded). Add in layers: Celery, green peppers, onion, and frozen peas. Spread on top 1 pint of mayonnaise. Sprinkle sugar on top of mayonnaise and cover top with shredded cheddar or Parmesan cheese and add crumbled bacon on top (or bacon bits). Cover with plastic wrap and refrigerate for 8 hours.

Serves: 18

1/2 head of lettuce shredded
1/2 cup celery
1/2 cup green pepper
1/2 cup onion
10 ounces peas, frozen
1 pint mayonnaise
2 tablespoons sugar
4 ounces cheddar cheese, shredded
8 slices bacon strip, crumbled

Nutritional Values:
Per Serving (excluding unknown items): 663 Calories; 71g Fat (91.1% calories from fat); 7g Protein; 9g Carbohydrate; 2g Dietary Fiber; 50mg Cholesterol; 1297mg Sodium.
Points: 19

Substitute Values:
Per Serving (using fat-free mayonnaise, sour cream and fat-free cheddar cheese): 65 Calories; 1g Fat (20.3% calories from fat); 4g Protein; 9g Carbohydrate; 1g Dietary Fiber; 4mg Cholesterol; 451mg Sodium.
Points: 1

Taco Salad

Crumble hamburger and cook in skillet. Drain fat from hamburger. Add rest of ingredients and toss.

Servings: 4
Start to finish: 30 minutes

1 pound ground beef, cooked and drained
1 head lettuce, iceberg
1 small kidney beans, canned
1 avocado, chopped
1 small olives, sliced
8 ounces tortilla chips
1 whole tomato
1 thousand island salad dressing
1 stalk celery, chopped

Nutritional Values:
Per Serving (excluding unknown items): 682 Calories; 42g Fat (54.9% calories from fat); 33g Protein; 45g Carbohydrate; 16g Dietary Fiber; 96mg Cholesterol; 201mg Sodium.
Points: 16

Substitute Values:
Per Serving (using thousand island salad dressing. low cal, ground beef, extra lean, and reduce amount of tortilla chips to 2 oz.): 596 Calories; 32g Fat (46.9% calories from fat); 36g Protein; 45g Carbohydrate; 16g Dietary Fiber; 78mg Cholesterol; 199mg Sodium.
Points: 14

Frito Salad

Melt taco sauce and Velveeta together. Cook hamburger, onion, bell pepper, garlic, celery, and chili powder, drain. In a salad bowl mix lettuce and tomato. Add Frito to salad mix. Next pour meat mixture on Frito and the melted cheese over it. Yum!
Serve with favorite bread or garlic bread.

Servings: 4
Start to finish: 30 minutes

1 pound ground beef
1/2 cup taco sauce, 1/2 of canned
1 pound Velveeta
1 small onion, diced
1 clove garlic, diced
1 stalk celery, diced
2 tablespoons chili powder
1 head lettuce, shredded
2 whole tomato, diced
28 grams Frito's, corn chips

Nutritional Values:
Per Serving (excluding unknown items): 912 Calories; 64g Fat (61.3% calories from fat); 59g Protein; 32g Carbohydrate; 4g Dietary Fiber; 220mg Cholesterol; 3216mg Sodium.
Points: 23

Substitute Values:
Per Serving (using extra lean ground beef, reduced fat Velveeta, and baked tortilla chips): 345 Calories; 21g Fat (58.6% calories from fat); 23g Protein; 11g Carbohydrate; 4g Dietary Fiber; 78mg Cholesterol; 311mg Sodium.
Points: 8

Sauerkraut Salad

Drain 1 large can of Sauerkraut and add onion, green pepper, carrots, pimento(optional), celery in mixing bowl. Combine vinegar, sugar, oil and celery seed in a sauce pan and bring to boil. Then pour hot dressing over Sauerkraut mixture, toss and refrigerate. This keeps well and is very delicious.

Servings: 4
Start to finish: 20 minutes

1 large sauerkraut, canned or fresh
1/2 cup onion, chopped
1/2 cup green pepper, chopped
1/2 cup carrot, grated
1/2 cup pimiento, optional
1/2 cup celery, diced
1/4 cup vinegar
1 cup sugar
1/4 cup oil
1 tablespoon celery seed

Nutritional Values:
Per Serving (excluding unknown items): 357 Calories; 14g Fat (34.5% calories from fat); 2g Protein; 59g Carbohydrate; 3g Dietary Fiber; 0mg Cholesterol; 414mg Sodium.
Points: 8

Substitute Values:
Per Serving (using sugar substitute and Canola oil or olive oil): 257 Calories; 14g Fat (49.6% calories from fat); 1g Protein; 31g Carbohydrate; 3g Dietary Fiber; 0mg Cholesterol; 508mg Sodium.
Points: 6

Dutch Lunch Salad

Mix all ingredients except green olives. Cover lightly with French (Basic French Dressing page 53), dressing and toss carefully. Let stand overnight, or refrigerate at least 6 hours. Salt to taste. Add some mayonnaise to moisten. Garnish with olives.

Servings: 6
Start to finish: 45 minutes

1 cup sauerkraut , raw
1 cup macaroni, cooked, elbow
1 cup ham slice, diced, can use boiled
1/2 cup cheddar cheese, diced
1/4 cup sweet pickle, chopped
1 cup celery, chopped
1/4 cup green onions, minced
1/2 cup green pepper, chopped
1/8 cup pimento, chopped

Nutritional Values:
Per Serving (excluding unknown items): 128 Calories; 6g Fat (40.1% calories from fat); 8g Protein; 11g Carbohydrate; 1g Dietary Fiber; 23mg Cholesterol; 439mg Sodium.
Points: 3

Substitute Values:
Per Serving (using fat-free ham slices and fat free cheddar cheese): 97 Calories; trace Fat (2.2% calories from fat); 12g Protein; 11g Carbohydrate; 1g Dietary Fiber; 23mg Cholesterol; 686mg Sodium.
Points: 2

Six Weeks Cabbage

Chop and mix together cabbage, green pepper, pimento, and onion. Boil together in saucepan vinegar, sugar, mustard seed, salt, celery seed and turmeric. Pour boiling liquid over chopped vegetable. Cool, cover and refrigerate. This will keep six weeks and is great as a salad with ham.

Servings: 14
Start to finish: 45 minutes

3 quarts Cabbage
1 whole green pepper, large
1 whole pimento, large
4 whole onion, medium
1 quart vinegar
2 1/2 cups sugar substitute
1 teaspoon mustard seed
1 teaspoon salt
1/2 teaspoon celery seed
1/2 teaspoon turmeric

Nutritional Values:
Per Serving (excluding unknown items): 183 Calories; trace Fat (1.7% calories from fat); 2g Protein; 47g Carbohydrate; 3g Dietary Fiber; 0mg Cholesterol; 168mg Sodium.
Points: 3

Substitute Values:
Per Serving (using sugar substitute): 113 Calories; trace Fat (2.9% calories from fat); 2g Protein; 27g Carbohydrate; 3g Dietary Fiber; 0mg Cholesterol; 237mg Sodium.
Points: 2

Orange Endive Salad

Combine and mix together lettuce, endive, mandarin orange, and onion. In separate mixing bowl, whisk together parsley, olive oil, wine vinegar and salt and pepper. Mix well and pour over salad mixture

Servings: 6
Start to finish: 20 minutes

1/2 head head lettuce
1/2 pound endive
2 cups mandarin orange, drained
1 whole onion, medium
2 tablespoons parsley, diced
3 tablespoons olive oil
1 tablespoon wine vinegar
salt and pepper, to taste

Nutritional Values:
Per Serving (excluding unknown items): 94 Calories; 7g Fat (62.7% calories from fat); 1g Protein; 8g Carbohydrate; 2g Dietary Fiber; 0mg Cholesterol; 9mg Sodium..
Points: 2

Marinated Carrot Salad

Cook carrots in salted water until done, but still firm. Mix sugar, salad oil, dry mustard. onion, vinegar, salt, celery seed and green pepper. Pour over carrots and refrigerate for 24 hours.

Servings: 8
Start to finish: 2:45 minutes

2 pounds carrots ,
sliced 1/2" thick, boiled al dente'
1/2 cup sugar
1/2 cup salad oil
1/2 teaspoon dry mustard
1 whole onion, chopped
1/2 cup vinegar
1 teaspoon salt
1/2 teaspoon celery seed
1 whole green pepper, chopped

Nutritional Values:
Per Serving (excluding unknown items): 181 Calories; 14g Fat (66.0% calories from fat); trace Protein; 16g Carbohydrate; 1g Dietary Fiber; 0mg Cholesterol; 268mg Sodium.
Points: 5

Substitute Values:
Per Serving (using sugar substitute and Enova oil): 37 Calories; trace Fat (5.5% calories from fat); trace Protein; 9g Carbohydrate; 1g Dietary Fiber; 0mg Cholesterol; 292mg Sodium.
Points: 1

Marinated Zucchini Salad

In a shallow dish, combine carrots, zucchini and hearts of palm(canned). In screw top jar combine oil, vinegar, garlic, sugar, salt, mustard, and pepper. Cover and shake well. Pour over vegetables.
Chill several hours or overnight. To serve drain off marinade, arrange vegetables on individual plates on lettuce and top each with blue, Parmesan or cheddar cheese.

Servings: 8
Start to finish: 4 hours

16 ounces carrots, drained
2 cups raw zucchini, thinly sliced
14 ounces hearts of palm, canned, drained and sliced in thick pieces
2/3 cup salad oil
1/4 cup vinegar
1 clove garlic, minced
1 teaspoon sugar
3/4 teaspoon salt
3/4 teaspoon dry mustard
1 dash ground pepper
6 lettuce leaves, Bib
2 ounces blue cheese, crumbled, Parmesan or cheddar cheese, as garnish

Nutritional Values:
Per Serving (excluding unknown items): 266 Calories; 20g Fat (65.8% calories from fat); 4g Protein; 20g Carbohydrate; 3g Dietary Fiber; 5mg Cholesterol; 325mg Sodium.
Points: 6

Substitute Values:
Per Serving (using sugar substitute and canola oil): 265 Calories; 20g Fat (65.4% calories from fat); 4g Protein; 20g Carbohydrate; 3g Dietary Fiber; 5mg Cholesterol; 326mg Sodium.
Points: 6

Louie Sauce
(for shrimp or crab)

Mix whipping cream until stiff. Combine mayonnaise, ketchup (or chili sauce), lemon juice, Worcestershire sauce, sweet pickle and add to whipped cream. Mix well and chill. Serve over shrimp or crab.

Servings: 6
Start to finish: 1:20 minutes

1 cup mayonnaise
3 tablespoons ketchup, or chili sauce
1 teaspoon lemon juice
1 teaspoon Worcestershire sauce
2 tablespoons sweet pickle, chopped
12 tablespoons whipped cream

Nutritional Values:
Per Serving (excluding unknown items): 150 Calories; 15g Fat (85.9% calories from fat); 1g Protein; 4g Carbohydrate; trace Dietary Fiber; 54mg Cholesterol; 145mg Sodium.
Points: 4

Substitute Values:
Per Serving (using fat-free mayonnaise, fat free cool whip ready made): 45 Calories; trace Fat (0.6% calories from fat); trace Protein; 11g Carbohydrate; trace Dietary Fiber; 0mg Cholesterol; 636mg Sodium.
Points: 1

French Dressing

Mix first 7 ingredients and let stand for several hours. Stir occasionally. Remove onions and add soup., chili sauce, and egg yolk. Mix well. Store in refrigerator. Keeps indefinitely.

Servings: 25
Serving size: 2 tablespoons
Start to finish: 3:30 minutes

1 1/8 cups canola oil
1/2 cup vinegar
1/2 cup sugar substitute
1/2 cup onion, quartered
1/2 teaspoon paprika
1/4 teaspoon dry mustard
1 1/8 teaspoons salt
4 1/2 fluid ounces tomato soup, undiluted
1/2 cup chili sauce
1/2 egg, yolk

Nutritional Values:
Per Serving (excluding unknown items): 102 Calories; 10g Fat (85.8% calories from fat); trace Protein; 3g Carbohydrate; trace Dietary Fiber; 5mg Cholesterol; 122mg Sodium.
Points: 4

Substitute Values:
Per Serving (using sugar substitute and olive or canola oil): 92 Calories; 10g Fat (92.7% calories from fat); trace Protein; 1g Carbohydrate; trace Dietary Fiber; 5mg Cholesterol; 113mg Sodium.
Points: 3

Garlic Salad Dressing

Combine dry ingredients in mixing bowl Then add salad oil and wine vinegar and mix well. Serve over salad. Store covered.

Servings: 24
Start to finish: 10 minutes

1 cup water
8 teaspoons bitters
2 tablespoons garlic salt
2 tablespoons sugar substitute
2 teaspoons cumin
4 tablespoons Worcestershire sauce
2 teaspoons oregano
2 teaspoons garlic powder
2 teaspoons accent® seasoning
1 teaspoon pepper
1 1/2 cups olive oil
1/2 cup wine vinegar

Nutritional Values:
Per Serving (excluding unknown items): 131 Calories; 14g Fat (92.0% calories from fat); trace Protein; 3g Carbohydrate; trace Dietary Fiber; 0mg Cholesterol; 588mg Sodium.
Points: 4

Substitute Values:
Per Serving (using sugar substitute and olive oil): 128 Calories; 14g Fat (93.6% calories from fat); trace Protein; 2g Carbohydrate; trace Dietary Fiber; 0mg Cholesterol; 590mg Sodium.
Points: 4

VEGETABLES AND SIDE DISHES

VEGETABLES AND SIDE DISHES

String Bean Casserole

Cook bean a little less than directions. Place half in casserole dish, then layer with half the can of sprouts, half the water chestnuts, and half the soup and cheese to cover. Then another layer of each and topped with half cheese. Bake at 350 degrees for ½ hour. When done add onions on top.

Servings: 4
Start to finish: 30 minutes

2 packages frozen string beans
(not French cut)
1 can bean sprouts
1 can water chestnuts
1 can cream of mushroom soup
1 can French fried onions
Grated cheddar cheese

Nutritional Values:
Per Serving (excluding unknown items): 251 Calories; 14g Fat (49.0% calories from fat); 14g Protein; 20g Carbohydrate; 6g Dietary Fiber; 40mg Cholesterol; 421mg Sodium.
Points: 8

Substitute Values:
Per Serving (using cream of mushroom low sodium and fat-free cheddar cheese): 131 Calories; trace Fat (1.7% calories from fat); 16g Protein; 19g Carbohydrate; 6g Dietary Fiber; 7mg Cholesterol; 285mg Sodium.
Points: 2

Portuguese Beans

Melt butter in sauce pan and add flour salt sugar pepper sour cream onion and add to the sauce and stir. Add cooked frozen French cut greens beans to sauce. Place in a baking dish and cover beans with ½ lb. Grated cheddar cheese. Top with mixture of crushed cornflakes and melted butter (enough to moisten). Bake 350° until hot and bubbly.

Servings: 4
Start to finish: 30 minutes

3 tablespoons melted butter
2 teaspoons flour
1 teaspoon salt
1 teaspoon sugar
1 dash pepper
1 cup sour cream
18 ounces green beans,
(cooked French cut)
1/2 pound grated cheddar cheese
2 cups cornflake , crushed

Nutritional Values:
Per Serving (excluding unknown items): 472 Calories; 40g Fat (73.9% calories from fat); 18g Protein; 13g Carbohydrate; 4g Dietary Fiber; 108mg Cholesterol; 1010mg Sodium.
Points: 12

Substitute Values:
Per Serving (using sugar substitute and olive oil): 199 Calories; 4g Fat (18.7% calories from fat); 25g Protein; 18g Carbohydrate; 4g Dietary Fiber; 17mg Cholesterol; 1094mg Sodium.
Points: 4

Broad Beans

Fry diced bacon until crisp and set to one side.
Clean beans and snap in two or they can be left in long pieces. Cook in salted water till tender, 15-20 min. (longer and they lose color). Drain well, add cream, pepper (use white pepper) and nutmeg. Keep warm. Add bacon and toss when ready.

Servings: 4
Start to finish: 30 minutes

1 pound green beans, fresh
salt and pepper, to season
1/8 teaspoon nutmeg, to season
1/2 cup bacon strips (4 strips)
2 tablespoons sour cream

Nutritional Values:
Per Serving (excluding unknown items): 47 Calories; 2g Fat (28.0% calories from fat); 2g Protein; 7g Carbohydrate; 3g Dietary Fiber; 3mg Cholesterol; 10mg Sodium.
Points: 1

Substitute Values:
Per Serving (using sugar substitute and olive oil): 36 Calories; trace Fat (2.9% calories from fat); 2g Protein; 8g Carbohydrate; 3g Dietary Fiber; 1mg Cholesterol; 11mg Sodium.
Points: 0

Bean Sprouts
(for Microwave)

Rinse bean sprouts in water. Microwave sprouts in plastic bag tied with a string on high 2 min. Drain excess fluid. In a separate microwavable 2 qt. Bowl add peanut oil and microwave on high for 2 min. Add bean sprouts, salt, soy sauce, and green onions toss to blend flavors.

Servings: 4
Start to finish: 10 minutes

4 cups bean sprouts, 2/3 lb.
2 tablespoons peanut oil
1/2 teaspoon salt
1/8 teaspoon soy sauce
1 stalk green onion, chopped

Nutritional Values:
Per Serving (excluding unknown items): 92 Calories; 7g Fat (61.7% calories from fat); 3g Protein; 6g Carbohydrate; 2g Dietary Fiber; 0mg Cholesterol; 284mg Sodium.
Points: 2

Company Beets with Pineapple

2 tablespoons brown sugar
1 tablespoon cornstarch
1/4 teaspoon salt
9 ounces pineapple chunks in juice, diced
1 tablespoon butter
1 tablespoon lemon juice
1 pound beets, canned, sliced

Combine first 3 ingredients in saucepan; stir in pineapple. Cook, stirring constantly, until thick and bubbly. Add butter, lemon juice and beets. Heat through.

Servings: 4
Start to finish: 30 minutes

Nutritional Values:
Per Serving (excluding unknown items): 124 Calories; 3g Fat (21.0% calories from fat); 1g Protein; 25g Carbohydrate; 2g Dietary Fiber; 8mg Cholesterol; 385mg Sodium.
Points: 2

Substitute Values:
Per Serving (using substitute brown sugar Splenda substitute and margarine, imitation): 132 Calories; 2g Fat (14.3% calories from fat); 1g Protein; 20g Carbohydrate; 2g Dietary Fiber; 0mg Cholesterol; 389mg Sodium.
Points: 2

Bozzo Beans

Combine ingredients and Bake in casserole dish at 350° for 1-1 1/2 hours. You can always add more beans. You can't ruin this recipe.

Servings: 8
Start to finish: 1:30 minutes

16 ounces baked beans, canned
13 ounces chili, canned
8 ounces tomato , canned
1/2 cup onion, chopped
1/2 cup green pepper, chopped
1/4 teaspoon salt
1/4 teaspoon garlic powder
1/4 teaspoon pepper
1 tablespoon cumin
1 tablespoon oregano
1 1/2 cups cheese, jack cheese for top

Nutritional Values:
Per Serving (excluding unknown items): 116 Calories; 3g Fat (21.4% calories from fat); 6g Protein; 19g Carbohydrate; 6g Dietary Fiber; 8mg Cholesterol; 534mg Sodium.
Points: 2

Beer Beans

Cook all ingredients one at a time and set aside. Pour off excess fat. In large pan combine Kidney beans (drained), tomato soup, and beer. Add all ingredients together and sprinkle with Parmesan cheese on top. Bake in slow oven 250° for 2-3 hours.

Servings: 8
Start to finish: 2-3 hours
Serve with green salad, French bread and wine.

1/4 pound bacon broken up
1/2 whole onion, white
1 pound ground beef (If you like spicy add skinned hot Italian sausage crumbled 4-5 links)
16 1/2 ounces kidney beans, canned, 2-3 15oz canned
16 1/2 ounces tomato soup (same size as beans) undiluted
12 fluid ounces beer your choice
Parmesan cheese, topping

Nutritional Values:
Per Serving (excluding unknown items): 346 Calories; 23g Fat (61.1% calories from fat); 17g Protein; 15g Carbohydrate; 2g Dietary Fiber; 60mg Cholesterol; 637mg Sodium.
Points: 15

Substitute Values:
Per Serving (using substitute bacon pieces reduced fat, ground beef, 95% lean and light beer): 287 Calories; 5g Fat (27.6% calories from fat); 15g Protein; 14g Carbohydrate; 2g Dietary Fiber; 26mg Cholesterol; 895mg Sodium.
Points: 6

Broccoli Supreme

Cook Rice as directed. Cook Broccoli chop and drain. Saute' onion and celery until tender. Combine all ingredients and bake at 350° for ½ hour.

Servings: 6
Start to finish: 45 minutes

1 cup rice
32 ounces broccoli, frozen 2 pkg
1 whole onion, chopped
2 stalks celery, chopped
1/2 cup cheese whiz
10 ounces cream of chicken soup
1 dash tabasco sauce
salt and pepper, to taste

Nutritional Values:
Per Serving (excluding unknown items): 171 Calories; 2g Fat (10.3% calories from fat); 6g Protein; 33g Carbohydrate; 4g Dietary Fiber; 2mg Cholesterol; 230mg Sodium.
Points: 3

Substitute Values:
Per Serving (using substitute): 148 Calories; 1g Fat (3.5% calories from fat); 5g Protein; 32g Carbohydrate; 4g Dietary Fiber; 0mg Cholesterol; 40mg Sodium.
Points: 2

Broccoli Quiche

Using your favorite pastry recipe or store bought shell. Bake pastry shell at 450 degrees , remove from oven and sprinkle with Parmesan cheese.
Layer half broccoli, then swiss cheese and onions and repeat until pie crust is full. Combine eggs, chicken broth, half and half, salt and Tabasco sauce. Pour liquid mix over all. Sprinkle with Parmesan cheese. Bake 10 min. 450 degrees then reduce heat to 325° for 20 min.

Servings: 6

Half and half substitute recipe:
7/8 cup milk
7/8 tablespoon melted butter, cooled combine and pour your desired measurement

Start to finish: 45 minutes

1/4 cup Parmesan cheese
2 cups broccoli, cleaned & quartered
1 cup swiss cheese, shredded
1/4 cup onion
3 whole egg
2/3 cup chicken broth
1/2 cup half and half
1/2 teaspoon salt
1/4 teaspoon tabasco sauce

Nutritional Values:
Per Serving (excluding unknown items): 163 Calories; 11g Fat (61.9% calories from fat); 12g Protein; 4g Carbohydrate; 1g Dietary Fiber; 133mg Cholesterol; 424mg Sodium.
Points: 4

Substitute Values:
Per Serving (using fat-free Parmesan cheese, fat-free Swiss cheese, milk, 1% low fat, and butter substitute): 119 Calories; 5g Fat (36.3% calories from fat); 12g Protein; 7g Carbohydrate; 1g Dietary Fiber; 119mg Cholesterol; 625mg Sodium.
Points: 3

Anise Carrots

Stir-fry carrots in margarine till just tender. Add water, salt and pepper. Steam for several minutes. Add cream and anise.

Servings: 4
Start to finish: 20 minutes

Heavy Cream Substitute:
1/8 cup milk, 1% low fat
1/16 cup margarine, imitation, melted and cooled
Combine milk and pour into cooled butter and measure desired amount.

2 tablespoons butter
4 cups carrot, sliced
3 tablespoons water
3 tablespoons heavy cream
1/2 teaspoon anise seed
salt and pepper, to taste

Nutritional Values:
Per Serving (excluding unknown items): 95 Calories; 4g Fat (39.6% calories from fat); 2g Protein; 13g Carbohydrate; 4g Dietary Fiber; 15mg Cholesterol; 50mg Sodium.
Points: 4

Substitute Values:
Per Serving (using heavy cream substitute): 71 Calories; 2g Fat (20.1% calories from fat); 2g Protein; 14g Carbohydrate; 4g Dietary Fiber; trace Cholesterol; 84mg Sodium.
Points: 1

Tangy Mustard Cauliflower

(For the Microwave)

Place whole cauliflower and water in 1 ½ qt. Glass casserole. Cover with glass lid. Microwave on high for 9 min. Drain. Combine in a small mixing bowl. Spoon mustard sauce on top of cauliflower. Sprinkle over cauliflower. Microwave for 1 ½ to 2 min. on roast to heat topping and melt cheese. Let stand 2 min. before serving. Can cook ahead of time.

Servings: 8
Start to finish: 15 minutes

1 medium cauliflower
1/4 cup water
1/2 cup mayonnaise, or salad dressing of your choice
1 teaspoon onion, finely chopped
1 teaspoon prepared mustard
1/4 teaspoon salt
1/2 cup swiss cheese, shredded

Nutritional Values:
Per Serving (excluding unknown items): 129 Calories; 14g Fat (90.0% calories from fat); 2g Protein; 1g Carbohydrate; trace Dietary Fiber; 11mg Cholesterol; 175mg Sodium.
Points: 4

Substitute Values:
Per Serving (using substitute fat-free mayonnaise and fat-free swiss cheese): 26 Calories; trace Fat (1.9% calories from fat); 2g Protein; 4g Carbohydrate; trace Dietary Fiber; 1mg Cholesterol; 362mg Sodium.
Points: 0

Almond Vegetables Mandarin

Cook and stir carrots and beans with oil in skillet over medium high heat for 2 min. Add Zucchini and onion; cook 1 min. longer. Add mix of water bouillon cube, cornstarch and garlic. Cook and stir until thickened. Vegetables should be crisp and tender. If they need further cooking, reduce heat, cover and steam till done. Add almonds.

Servings: 6
Start to finish: 45 minutes

1 cup carrots, thinly sliced
1 cup green beans, cut 1" thick
2 tablespoons salad oil
1 cup zucchini, thinly sliced
1/2 cup green onion, sliced
1 cup water
1 chicken bouillon cube
2 teaspoons garlic powder
1/2 cup almonds, whole and un-blanched

Nutritional Values:
Per Serving (excluding unknown items): 135 Calories; 11g Fat (68.2% calories from fat); 4g Protein; 8g Carbohydrate; 3g Dietary Fiber; trace Cholesterol; 137mg Sodium.
Points: 3

Substitute Values:
Per Serving (using olive oil and half almonds substitute): 61 Calories; 3g Fat (46.1% calories from fat); 2g Protein; 7g Carbohydrate; 2g Dietary Fiber; trace Cholesterol; 136mg Sodium.
Points: 1

French Mushrooms

Saute' onion in butter until tender. Stir in mushrooms. Cover and cook until mushroom are tender. Add salt, paprika, pepper and sour cream. Serve sprinkled with parsley.

Servings: 6
Start to finish: 20 minutes

1 cup onions, chopped
1/4 cup butter
1 pound fresh mushrooms, sliced
1 teaspoon salt
1 teaspoon pepper
1 cup sour cream
1 cup parsley, chopped

Nutritional Values:
Per Serving (excluding unknown items): 183 Calories; 16g Fat (75.7% calories from fat); 3g Protein; 8g Carbohydrate; 2g Dietary Fiber; 38mg Cholesterol; 463mg Sodium.
Points: 5

Substitute Values:
Per Serving (using margarine, imitation and fat free sour cream substitute): 92 Calories; 4g Fat (37.2% calories from fat); 5g Protein; 11g Carbohydrate; 2g Dietary Fiber; 4mg Cholesterol; 486mg Sodium.
Points: 2

Baked Zucchini

Saute onion and garlic in oil in frying pan. Add diced zucchini. Salt and pepper to taste. When zucchini becomes slightly transparent add 4 to 6 beaten eggs(enough to cover the vegetables). Place in casserole and spread grated cheese over the top. Put in 275° oven until eggs are set.

Servings: 4
Start to finish: 30 minutes

1 whole onion , chopped
1 clove garlic, chopped
salt and pepper, to taste
6 eggs, beaten
1 1/2 cups grated cheddar cheese

Nutritional Values:
Per Serving (excluding unknown items): 189 Calories; 14g Fat (69.3% calories from fat); 13g Protein; 1g Carbohydrate; trace Dietary Fiber; 242mg Cholesterol; 246mg Sodium.
Points: 5

Substitute Values:
Per Serving (using substitute): 115 Calories; 5g Fat (39.7% calories from fat); 15g Protein; 2g Carbohydrate; trace Dietary Fiber; 217mg Cholesterol; 273mg Sodium.
Points: 3

Oven Friend Potatoes

Arrange potato wedges, peel side down in shallow baking pan. Brush oil mixture over potatoes. Bake in preheated oven 375° oven for 45 min. or until potatoes are golden brown and tender, brushing occasionally with oil mixture.

Servings: 4
Start to finish: 1 hour

8 large potato, leave peel on
and cut into wedges
1/2 cup olive oil
2 tablespoons Parmesan cheese
1 teaspoon salt
1/2 teaspoon garlic powder
1/2 teaspoon paprika
1/4 teaspoon pepper

Nutritional Values:
Per Serving (excluding unknown items): 447 Calories; 28g Fat (55.7% calories from fat); 6g Protein; 44g Carbohydrate; 4g Dietary Fiber; 2mg Cholesterol; 594mg Sodium.
Points: 10

Substitute Values:
Per Serving (using enova cooking oil and fat free Parmesan cheese): 206 Calories; 1g Fat (2.2% calories from fat); 6g Protein; 46g Carbohydrate; 4g Dietary Fiber; 3mg Cholesterol; 575mg Sodium.
Points: 3

Microwave Hollandaise Sauce

Combine ingrdients in sauce pan and cook on high for 15 sec. Whip. Cook again 15 sec. Whip.

Servings: 4
Start to finish: 30 minutes

1/4 cup butter
2 teaspoon lemon juice
2 egg yolks
2 tablespoons evaporated milk – whip

Nutritional Values:
Per Serving (excluding unknown items): 48 Calories; 3g Fat (58.6% calories from fat); 4g Protein; 1g Carbohydrate; trace Dietary Fiber; 108mg Cholesterol; 43mg Sodium.
Points: 1

Substitute Values:
Per Serving (using evaporated skim milk substitute): 44 Calories; 3g Fat (52.6% calories from fat); 4g Protein; 1g Carbohydrate; trace Dietary Fiber; 106mg Cholesterol; 44mg Sodium..
Points: 1

Au Gratin Potatoes

Mix and bake in a 9"x9"at 325° for 1 hour.

Servings: 4
Start to finish: 30 minutes

1 pound hash browns, frozen
10 1/2 ounces cheddar cheese soup
12 ounces evaporated milk
6 ounces French fried Onions, half mixed in and half on top.

Nutritional Values:
Per Serving (excluding unknown items): 208 Calories; 7g Fat (30.5% calories from fat); 8g Protein; 29g Carbohydrate; 2g Dietary Fiber; 25mg Cholesterol; 115mg Sodium.
Points: 6

Substitute Values:
Per Serving (using substitute evaporated skimmed milk): 160 Calories; 1g Fat (5.1% calories from fat); 9g Protein; 30g Carbohydrate; 2g Dietary Fiber; 3mg Cholesterol; 123mg Sodium
Points: 3

Funny Spaghetti
(Good with BBQ Ribs or Chicken)

Put 2 to 3 tablespoons oil in a pan with a clove of garlic. Add cooked spaghetti and stir in all of the above. Good, and very colorful on the plate.

Servings: 4
Start to finish: 30 minutes

2/3 cup walnuts, chopped
1/2 cup black olive, chopped
1/2 cup pimento, not packed in vinegar
1/3 cup parsley, chopped
1 teaspoon basil
salt and pepper, to taste
1 ounce spaghetti, cooked and drained

Nutritional Values:
Per Serving (excluding unknown items): 175 Calories; 14g Fat (66.3% calories from fat); 6g Protein; 9g Carbohydrate; 2g Dietary Fiber; 0mg Cholesterol; 151mg Sodium.
Points: 4

Holiday Mashed Potatoes

Add cream cheese in small lumps and the butter to mashed potatoes. Beat well. Add sour cream, eggs, milk, onions, salt and pepper to taste. Beat until fluffy. Place in casserole. Refrigerate for several hours or over night. Bake 45 min. at 350° until lightly browned on top.

Servings: 6
Start to finish: 3 hours 45 minutes

3 pounds Potatoes , peeled, quartered, cooked and mashed
8 ounces cream cheese, pkg
1/2 cup milk,
1/4 cup butter
12 ounces sour cream, small carton
2 whole eggs, lightly beaten
1/2 cup onion, finely chopped
1 teaspoon salt
dash pepper

Nutritional Values:
Per Serving (excluding unknown items): 363 Calories; 35g Fat (85.6% calories from fat); 8g Protein; 6g Carbohydrate; trace Dietary Fiber; 161mg Cholesterol; 609mg Sodium.
Points: 10

Substitute Values:
Per Serving (using fat-free cream cheese, skim milk, fat-free sour cream and Egg Beaters® 99% egg substitute substitute): 167 Calories; 8g Fat (43.6% calories from fat); 13g Protein; 11g Carbohydrate; trace Dietary Fiber; 30mg Cholesterol; 745mg Sodium.
Points: 4

Mari's Potatoes

3 Medium size baking potatoes peeled and sliced ¼ in. thick. Spread out (as you would a deck of cards) in a flat baking dish. Cover with chicken broth. Sprinkle generously with Parmesan and paprika. Bake at 350° about 1 hour.

Servings: 4
Start to finish: 1:15 minutes

1 can chicken broth
3 medium size baking potatoes
Parmesan cheese
Paprika

Nutritional Values:
Per Serving (excluding unknown items): 61 Calories; 4g Fat (53.8% calories from fat); 6g Protein; 1g Carbohydrate; 0g Dietary Fiber; 8mg Cholesterol; 502mg Sodium.
Points: 2

Substitute Values:
Per Serving (using chicken broth low sodium and fat-free Parmesan cheese substitute): 36 Calories; trace Fat (0.0% calories from fat); 5g Protein; 5g Carbohydrate; 0g Dietary Fiber; 12mg Cholesterol; 108mg Sodium.
Points: 1

Sweet Potato and Apple Scallop

Slice the apples crosswise into thin slices (½ thick). In a large casserole, place a layer of potatoes which you have sliced crosswise into pieces about ½ -in. thick. Next, cover with sliced apples. Sprinkle thickly with cinnamon and sugar and dot with butter pieces.

Continue layering up the potatoes and apples with the cinnamon, sugar and butter. Mix the orange rind with the orange juice and pour over layered potatoes and apples. Bake at
350° for about 40 to 50 min. or until apples are tender.

Servings: 4
Start to finish: 1 hour

6 cups sweet potatoes , cooked and peeled or yams
4 cups apple, peeled and cored
3/4 cup sugar substitute
1 tablespoon cinnamon
2 tablespoons margarine, imitation, cut into pieces
rind of orange, grated
1/2 cup orange juice

Nutritional Values:
Per Serving (excluding unknown items): 112 Calories; 3g Fat (19.1% calories from fat); trace Protein; 24g Carbohydrate; 2g Dietary Fiber; 6mg Cholesterol; 24mg Sodium.
Points: 2

Substitute Values:
Per Serving (using substitute): 72 Calories; 1g Fat (16.4% calories from fat); trace Protein; 15g Carbohydrate; 2g Dietary Fiber; 0mg Cholesterol; 57mg Sodium.
Points: 1

Easy Rice Pilaf

Break vermicelli into inch lengths. Saute in hot butter until browned. Ass the rest of ingredients, cover and simmer till rice is done, about 25 min.

Serving Ideas: Add ¼ cup pine nuts or 1 teaspoon saffron. Diced tomatoes can be added the last few minutes of cooking time.

Servings: 4
Start to finish: 30 minutes

1/4 cup vermicelli
2 tablespoons butter
1/2 cup rice, uncooked
salt, to coat baking dish
1 teaspoon chicken bouillon, smash cube up
1 1/2 cups water

Nutritional Values:
Per Serving (excluding unknown items): 159 Calories; 6g Fat (34.0% calories from fat); 2g Protein; 24g Carbohydrate; trace Dietary Fiber; 16mg Cholesterol; 70mg Sodium.
Points: 4

Substitute Values:
Per Serving (using margarine imitation substitute): 133 Calories; 3g Fat (20.6% calories from fat); 2g Protein; 24g Carbohydrate; trace Dietary Fiber; 0mg Cholesterol; 81mg Sodium.
Points: 3

Green Rice

Saute in olive oil or butter onion and minced garlic. Add remaining ingredients to sauted mixture. Mix thoroughly. Pour into greased baking dish and bake about 40 min. at 350°.

Servings: 4
Start to finish: 60 minutes

3 tablespoons butter
2 tablespoons onion, chopped
1/4 teaspoon garlic, minced
1 1/2 cups rice, cooked
1/2 cup parsley, chopped
1 cup milk
1 teaspoon salt
1 teaspoon Worcestershire sauce
1 cup sharp cheddar cheese
2 whole eggs, slightly beaten

Nutritional Values:
Per Serving (excluding unknown items): 262 Calories; 12g Fat (40.1% calories from fat); 9g Protein; 30g Carbohydrate; 1g Dietary Fiber; 84mg Cholesterol; 441mg Sodium.
Points: 6

Substitute Values:
Per Serving (using substitutes butter for olive oil and fat-free cheddar cheese): 232 Calories; 8g Fat (29.9% calories from fat); 9g Protein; 31g Carbohydrate; 1g Dietary Fiber; 56mg Cholesterol; 419mg Sodium.
Points: 5

Native Rice

Butter 1 ½ qt. Casserole. Cut jack cheese in long strips. Mix sour cream and chilies. Layer rice, sour cream, jack cheese with rice. Ending on top. Bake at 350° for 30 min. until bubbly. Put grated cheese on top for the last 10 min.

Servings: 4
Start to finish: 40 minutes

1/2 pound Monterey jack cheese
1 pint sour cream
7 ounces green chile's, chopped
1 cup rice, cooked or 1 1/2 cooked brown rice
1/3 cup cheddar cheese, grated

Nutritional Values:
Per Serving (excluding unknown items): 680 Calories; 45g Fat (59.1% calories from fat); 24g Protein; 46g Carbohydrate; 1g Dietary Fiber; 111mg Cholesterol; 429mg Sodium.
Points: 17

Substitute Values:
Per Serving (using fat-free jack, fat-free cheddar cheese, and fat-free sour cream substitute): 274 Calories; trace Fat (1.3% calories from fat); 15g Protein; 54g Carbohydrate; 1g Dietary Fiber; 14mg Cholesterol; 158mg Sodium.
Points: 5

Cheese Grits

Cook grits until thick and then add oleo, eggs, milk, roll of Kraft garlic cheese. Mix well and place in greased casserole, then bake at 350° for 30 min. or until browned and puffy.

Servings: 4
Start to finish: 40 minutes

Serving Ideas: Notes: 1 (6 ounce) package kraft garlic cheese rolls (looks like a sausage link, sometimes hard to find, can use garlic powder and Velveeta or similar)

1 cup grits, 3 min
3 cups water, boiling
1/2 teaspoon salt
1/4 cup butter
4 whole eggs
1 cup milk, skim
6 ounces kraft garlic cheese roll

Nutritional Values:
Per Serving (excluding unknown items): 342 Calories; 17g Fat (45.3% calories from fat); 12g Protein; 34g Carbohydrate; 0g Dietary Fiber; 244mg Cholesterol; 491mg Sodium.
Points: 8

Substitute Values:
Per Serving (using substitute garlic powder and fat free Velveeta): 291 Calories; 11g Fat (35.2% calories from fat); 12g Protein; 34g Carbohydrate; 0g Dietary Fiber; 213mg Cholesterol; 517mg Sodium.
Points: 2

Egg and Sausage Bake

(assemble the night before)

Cook sausage meat in medium size skillet, stirring to break up pieces, until browned. Drain. In large bowl beat eggs, milk and seasonings until blended; stir in sausage. And remaining ingredients. Pour mixture in lightly greased 8 in. square baking pan; cover and refrigerate over night. Remove from refrigerator 1 hour before baking. Bake in preheated oven at 325° for 1 to 1 ½ hours until lightly browned and knife inserted comes out clean. Cool 10 min. before cutting.

Servings: 8
Start to finish: 2:30 minutes

1 pound pork sausage, crumbled
6 whole eggs, large
2 cups milk
1 1/2 teaspoons dry mustard
3/4 teaspoon salt
1/2 teaspoon pepper, freshly ground
1/4 teaspoon paprika
1/4 teaspoon nutmeg, ground
dash red pepper, ground
3 slices white bread, firm and cubed
4 ounces sharp cheddar cheese, shredded

Nutritional Values:
Per Serving (excluding unknown items): 414 Calories; 34g Fat (74.2% calories from fat); 18g Protein; 9g Carbohydrate; trace Dietary Fiber; 221mg Cholesterol; 799mg Sodium.
Points: 11

Substitute Values:
Per Serving (using substitute wheat bread, fat-free cheddar cheese, lean sausage. And skim milk): 288 Calories; 22g Fat (68.7% calories from fat); 15g Protein; 7g Carbohydrate; trace Dietary Fiber; 161mg Cholesterol; 651mg Sodium..
Points: 7

Prune Chutney

Mix sugar and vingar and bring to boil. Add remaining ingredients except prunes and mix well. Add prunes and simmer until thickened 1 hour or more. Pack in sterilized jars.

Servings: 24
Start to finish: 1:20 minutes

1 cup light brown sugar
3/4 cup cider vinegar
2 teaspoons salt
2 cloves garlic, sliced thin
1 large onion, sliced thin
1 cup ginger, preserved sliced thin
1 cup white raisins, seedles3 1/2 cups prunes, halved and seeded
1 cup sugar
1 1/2 teaspoons red pepper, crushed

Nutritional Values:
Per Serving (excluding unknown items): 129 Calories; trace Fat (2.2% calories from fat); 1g Protein; 33g Carbohydrate; 2g Dietary Fiber; 0mg Cholesterol; 182mg Sodium.
Points: 2

Cathy's Fettuccine

Cook noodles till tender in water and oil. Drain. Meanwhile melt butter in sauce pan. Add cheese, cream, beaten egg and blend until slightly thickened. Add noodles, nutmeg, salt and pepper and toss lightly. Serve with additional grated Parmesan cheese.

Servings: 4
Start to finish: 40 minutes

16 ounces fettuccine
1 tablespoon olive oil
1/4 pound butter
3/4 cup fat-free Parmesan cheese
1/2 cup half-and-half
1 whole egg
pinch nutmeg, generous
salt and pepper to taste

Nutritional Values:
Per Serving (excluding unknown items): 520 Calories; 25g Fat (43.3% calories from fat); 16g Protein; 58g Carbohydrate; 2g Dietary Fiber; 92mg Cholesterol; 368mg Sodium.
Points: 12

Substitute Values:
Per Serving (using fat -free Parmesan, egg substitute, fat-free sour cream, and Enova cooking oil): 405 Calories; 9g Fat (19.7% calories from fat); 16g Protein; 64g Carbohydrate; 2g Dietary Fiber; 12mg Cholesterol; 343mg Sodium.
Points: 8

MEATS AND MAIN MEALS

MEATS

Saddlebag Jerky

Trim all excess fat and tissue from meat. Arrange flat for slicing and semi freeze for easier cutting. Slice with the grain into strips ¼" thick. Combine all ingredients for marinade. Favorite flavors such as soy sauce, cumin, worcestershire, and whatever may be substituted. Marinate the meat for 45 min. turning often to bring all surfaces into contact.

Arrange strips on oven rack without over lapping. Pepper each side if desired. Set oven thermostat at the lowest possible setting, leave oven door cracked open enough to keep it from getting brittle. I usually leave it in oven over night.

Good jerky is still moist enough to be chewy. Jerky may be stored for several weeks in clean coffee cans with plastic lids. Don't be afraid of the amount of salt this recipe calls for- it's necessary to preserve the meat. The marinating time is fairly short.

Servings: 8
Start to finish: 60 minutes

2 1/2 pounds brisket, trimmed lean, cut to 1 ½ " thick
4 cups boiling water
1/2 cup salt
1 tablespoon tabasco sauce
1 tablespoon liquid Barbecue Smoke®
1/2 teaspoon garlic powder
1 tablespoon oregano

Nutritional Values:
Per Serving (excluding unknown items): 3 Calories; trace Fat (19.8% calories from fat); trace Protein; 1g Carbohydrate; trace Dietary Fiber; trace Cholesterol; 6413mg Sodium.
Points: 1

Mom's Oven BBQ'd Ribs

Place ribs in greased roasting pan. Bake uncovered at 350° for 45 min. Meanwhile in a sauce pan combine remaining ingredients. Bring to boil, cook for 1 min. Drain ribs. Pour sauce over ribs, cover and bake 1 ½ hours. Uncover and bake 30 min. longer, basting once.

Note: You can use your favorite BBQ sauce instead of seasonings.

Servings: 8
Start to finish: 2:45 minutes

4 pounds pork backribs
1 1/2 cups water
1 cup ketchup
1/3 cup Worcestershire sauce
1 teaspoon salt
1 teaspoon chili powder
1/2 teaspoon onion powder
1/8 teaspoon hot pepper, sauce

Nutritional Values:
Per Serving (excluding unknown items): 438 Calories; 33g Fat (69.0% calories from fat); 23g Protein; 10g Carbohydrate; trace Dietary Fiber; 114mg Cholesterol; 830mg Sodium..
Points: 11

Beer Baked Ham

5 lb. canned ham, cut crosswise
1 jar cloves
1 ½ cups brown sugar packed firmly
1 quart beer (and pour yourself a beer)

Preheat oven 325°. Cut crosswise sections on top of the ham and cover top with cloves ½ deep half an in apart. Place in oven for 30 min. After 30 min. remove ham and spread brown sugar on top of ham ½ in. thick. Return to oven 20 min, then pour 2 12 oz. Beer over the top of ham. Baste every 10 min. for 40 min. Remove and let stand for 5 min.

Nutritional Values:
Per Serving (excluding unknown items): 696 Calories; 38g Fat (51.5% calories from fat); 49g Protein; 32g Carbohydrate; 2g Dietary Fiber; 111mg Cholesterol; 3549mg Sodium.
Points: 17

Servings: 8
Start to finish: 90 minutes

Easy Beef Burgundy

Cut beef into cubes. Put all ingredients in a heavy casserole or dutch oven. Stir slightly to mix., then cover. Bake at 325° for 3 hours. Serve over rice, noodles or mashed potatoes. Leftovers are always better the next day.

Servings: 8
Start to finish: 3:30 minutes

3 pounds beef chuck or sirloin, remove all fat
1 package onion soup mix, no water
10 ounces celery soup, no water
10 ounces cream of mushroom soup, no water
1 cup red wine
1/2 pound mushrooms, added last 15 minutes of cooking

Nutritional Values:
Per Serving (excluding unknown items): 416 Calories; 28g Fat (65.1% calories from fat); 28g Protein; 6g Carbohydrate; 1g Dietary Fiber; 99mg Cholesterol; 692mg Sodium
Points: 10

Substitute Values:
Per Serving (using substitute lean roast, and 98% fat free mushroom soup): 34 Calories; trace Fat (13.9% calories from fat); 1g Protein; 4g Carbohydrate; 1g Dietary Fiber; trace Cholesterol; 366mg Sodium.
Points: 1

Barbecued Brisket

Rub in liquid smoke flavoring all over the brisket, add remainder of seasonings and marinate overnight or for at least several hours refrigerated. Wrap in foil and cook in oven at 300° for 4 hours.

Servings: 6
Start to finish: 6 Hours

4 pounds Beef, brisket, flat
1 cup barbecue sauce, Woody's
cooking sauce is best
1 teaspoon onion powder
2 teaspoons celery seed
1 teaspoon garlic salt
2 tablespoons liquid smoke flavoring
1/2 teaspoon salt
2 teaspoons Worcestershire sauce
2 teaspoons pepper

Nutritional Values:
Per Serving (excluding unknown items): 918 Calories; 73g Fat (72.5% calories from fat); 55g Protein; 7g Carbohydrate; 1g Dietary Fiber; 212mg Cholesterol; 1082mg Sodium.
Points: 24

Substitute Values:
Per Serving (using substitute Beef, brisket, flat half, separable lean and fat, trimmed): 41 Calories; 1g Fat (22.4% calories from fat); 1g Protein; 7g Carbohydrate; 1g Dietary Fiber; trace Cholesterol; 894mg Sodium.
Points: 1

Lobster Stuffed Tenderloin of Beef

Cut beef lengthwise to within ½ inch of bottom to butterfly. Place frozen lobster tails in boiling salted water to cover. Return to boiling, reduce heat and simmer 5 to 6 min. Carefully remove lobster from shells. Cut in half lengthwise. Place lobster end to end inside beef. Combine the melted butter and lemon juice. Drizzle on lobster. Close meat around lobster. Tie roast together with string at intervals of 1 inch.

Place on rack in shallow roasting pan. Roast in 425° oven 45 to 50 min. for rare. Use meat thermometer for best results. Lay bacon slices on top. Roast 5 min. more. In sauce pan cook green onion in the remaining butter over very low heat till tender. Add wine and garlic salt and heat through, stirring. To serve, slice roast, spoon on wine sauce. Garnish platter with fluted whole mushrooms and watercress, if desired.

Servings: 4
Start to finish: 60 minutes

4 lbs. whole beef tenderloin
2 to 4 oz. frozen lobster tails
1 tablespoon butter, melted
6 slices bacon, partially cooked
1/2 cup sliced green onion
1/2 cup dry white wine
(always when cooking with wine pour yourself a glass)
1/2 cup butter
1/8 teaspoon lemon juice

Nutritional Values:
Per Serving (excluding unknown items): 416 Calories; 28g Fat (65.1% calories from fat); 28g Protein; 6g Carbohydrate; 1g Dietary Fiber; 99mg Cholesterol; 692mg Sodium
Points: 10

Substitute Values:
Per Serving (using substitute lean roast, and 98% fat free mushroom soup): 34 Calories; trace Fat (13.9% calories from fat); 1g Protein; 4g Carbohydrate; 1g Dietary Fiber; trace Cholesterol; 366mg Sodium.
Points: 1

Corned beef

Simmer corned beef in water and add all ingredients (except cloves) in pot and pour in enough water to cover meat. Remove before completely cooked. Dot with whole cloves. Place in roasting pan and bake at 350°, using sauce basting frequently, until done using meat thermometer.

Servings: 6
Start to finish: 3:00 minutes

2 1/4 pounds corned beef brisket, whole
3 cloves garlic, crushed
2 onions, medium, sliced
2 carrot, sliced
1 teaspoon dill seed
8 whole cloves
2 bay leaf
1/2 teaspoon rosemary

Baste frequently sauce:
2 tablespoon butter
1 tablespoon prepared mustard
1/3 cup brown sugar
5 tablespoons ketchup
3 tablespoons vinegar

Nutritional Values:
Per Serving (excluding unknown items): 435 Calories; 24g Fat (47.7% calories from fat); 23g Protein; 36g Carbohydrate; 7g Dietary Fiber; 76mg Cholesterol; 487mg Sodium.
Points: 10

Substitute Values:
Per Serving (using substitute corned beef brisket lean): 157 Calories; 3g Fat (15.5% calories from fat); 3g Protein; 36g Carbohydrate; 7g Dietary Fiber; 0mg Cholesterol; 316mg Sodium.
Points: 3

Dinner Beef En-Filo

Saute' onions in 2 tablespoons butter or margarine until transparent. Add mushrooms and meat.. Saute' until meat turns brown. Put in a large bowl, season with salt, pepper, oregano and garlic. Cool slightly. Add eggs, mix lightly, mix in cheese, parsley, crumbs and nuts. Chill.

Filo: Divide each sheet of silo in 3 equal strips, appropriately 5 inches wide. Brush two strips with melted butter, placing one on top of the other. At one end place 1/3 C meat mixture and fold up in a triangle like a flag fold. Place on a greased baking sheet. Repeat with remaining dough and filling. Butter top. May be frozen or baked at 400° for 15-20 min. Serve with 1 T sour cream mixed with dill on each. Cut small for hors d'oeuvre.

Servings: 8
Start to finish: 60 minutes

1 whole onion, small
2 tablespoons margarine
2 pounds mushroom, chopped
2 pounds ground beef
1 1/2 teaspoons salt
1/4 teaspoon pepper
1/2 teaspoon oregano
1/4 teaspoon garlic, finely chopped
1 1/2 cups parsley, minced
1/4 cup dry bread crumbs
1/2 cup walnuts chopped
1/2 pound filo, leaves
sour cream
dill relish

Nutritional Values:
Per Serving (excluding unknown items): 513 Calories; 35g Fat (69.7% calories from fat); 24g Protein; 10g Carbohydrate; 2g Dietary Fiber; 96mg Cholesterol; 688mg Sodium.
Points: 13

Substitute Values:
Per Serving (using extra lean beef, fat-free sour cream and no walnuts): 427 Calories; 25g Fat (60.0% calories from fat); 26g Protein; 10g Carbohydrate; 2g Dietary Fiber; 78mg Cholesterol; 685mg Sodium.
Points: 10

Pot Roast and Spaghetti

Brown pot roast. Remove from pot and lightly brown onion and garlic in drippings. Add tomatoes, tomato sauce, wine, salt, pepper, and oregano. When simmering, return meat to pot. Spoon sauce over and cook gently till meat is tender. (Thin with water or more wine if sauce gets too thick). When meat is tender, remove to heated platter and keep warm. Add cooked spaghetti to sauce; heat through and add mushrooms. Mound around roast on platter and sprinkle with grated cheese.

Servings: 8
Start to finish: 2:30 minutes

2 tablespoons oil
4 pounds roast, trimmed lean
1 whole onion, large, finely chopped
1 clove garlic, or more if needed
28 ounces tomato, canned
29 ounces tomato sauce
1 cup red wine
1/2 teaspoon salt and pepper
1/2 teaspoon oregano, to taste
1/2 pound fresh mushroom
1 pound spaghetti
Parmesan cheese, grated

Nutritional Values:
Per Serving (excluding unknown items): 325 Calories; 5g Fat (14.1% calories from fat); 10g Protein; 57g Carbohydrate; 4g Dietary Fiber; 0mg Cholesterol; 743mg Sodium.
Points: 6

Substitute Values:
Per Serving (using substitute Enova cooking oil): 300 Calories; 2g Fat (5.1% calories from fat); 11g Protein; 58g Carbohydrate; 4g Dietary Fiber; 2mg Cholesterol; 757mg Sodium.
Points: 5

Mom's Swedish Meatballs

Mix milk and crackers and let stand 15 min. Then add ketchup, paprika, salt, pepper and onion. Make 12 meatballs and Brown meatballs in 1 T bacon grease, slowly on low heat. When done set aside. Add mushroom gravy to Cracker mixture and heat in saucepan 15 min. Place meatballs in gravy and heat through.

Servings: 3
Start to finish: 40 minutes

1 pound beef ground extra lean
(makes 12 balls)
2/3 cup crackers, crushed
1/4 cup milk
1 tablespoon ketchup
1/4 teaspoon paprika
salt and pepper, to taste
1 whole onion, grated (optional)

Nutritional Values:
Per Serving (excluding unknown items): 546 Calories; 25g Fat (42.3% calories from fat); 34g Protein; 43g Carbohydrate; 2g Dietary Fiber; 97mg Cholesterol; 834mg Sodium.
Points: 13

Substitute Values:
Per Serving (using substitute ground beef, 95% lean and skim milk): 636 Calories; 10g Fat (25.4% calories from fat); 20g Protein; 43g Carbohydrate; 2g Dietary Fiber; 42mg Cholesterol; 800mg Sodium.
Points: 13

Pot Roast in Ale

Put Roast beef in a deep Crock pot. Pour over 3 bottles ale or beer. Add wine. Add water, if needed to cover roast. Salt and Pepper to taste. Marinate in refrigerator for at least 12 hours.

Drain and dry meat. Strain marinade and reserve.

Brown meat on all sides in margarine. Add ½ of marinade, 1 tsp. Caraway seeds and a bouquet garnish composed of sprig (or dried) thyme, rosemary, and 3 sprigs parsley. Cover pot and cook meat slowly for 3 hours or until tender. Add marinade as needed. Remove meat to hot platter. Discard bouquet and thicken sauce flour and margarine. Correct seasoning to taste and strain sauce into bowl to serve with roast.

Servings: 4
Start to finish: 15 hours

4 pounds sirloin tip roast, lean
36 ounces beer, Dark ale or beer
1/2 cup red wine
water, to cover meat
1 teaspoon caraway seeds
1 teaspoon thyme
1 teaspoon rosemary
3 sprigs parsley
1 tablespoon flour
1 tablespoon margarine

Nutritional Values:
Per Serving (excluding unknown items): 178 Calories; 3g Fat (30.2% calories from fat); 3g Protein; 15g Carbohydrate; 3g Dietary Fiber; 0mg Cholesterol; 91mg Sodium.
Points: 3

Viki's Meatloaf

Preheat oven at 350°. Butter loaf pans. Combine all ingredients in large bowl and mold into loaves (2). Pat into loaf pan(s) and bake for 45 min or until done using meat thermometer. Serve with A-1 or Worcestershire sauce.

Servings: 6
Start to finish: 1:30 minutes

2 pounds ground beef
salt and pepper, to taste
5 ounces seasoned bread stuffing mix
3/4 cup barbecue sauce or your favorite brand
2 whole eggs
1/4 cup milk
1 whole onion, chopped
1 whole bell pepper, chopped
1 tablespoon Worcestershire sauce

Nutritional Values:
Per Serving (excluding unknown items): 384 Calories; 31g Fat (74.7% calories from fat); 21g Protein; 3g Carbohydrate; 1g Dietary Fiber; 150mg Cholesterol; 118mg Sodium.
Points: 10

Substitute Values:
Per Serving (using substitute lean ground beef 95%, skim milk, and sugar free barbecue sauce): 318 Calories; 4g Fat (35.1% calories from fat); 13g Protein; 3g Carbohydrate; 1g Dietary Fiber; 84mg Cholesterol; 76mg Sodium.
Points: 6

Giant Stuffed Hamburger
(for your BBQ)

In medium saucepan melt margarine, remove from heat. Add stuffing mix, egg, mushrooms, beef broth, onion, almonds, parsley, and lemon juice; mix well and set aside. Combine ground beef and salt; divide meat in half. On sheets of waxed paper, pat each half to an 8 in. circle, spoon stuffing over one circle of meat to within 1 inch of edge. Top with second circle of meat; peel off top sheet of paper and seal edges. Invert meat patty on to a well greased grill basket; peel off remaining paper. Grill over medium coals. About 10 to 12 minutes or done to meat thermometer. Cut into wedges and serve with warm ketchup.

Servings: 6
Start to finish: 30 minutes

2 tablespoons margarine
1 ¼ cups herb seasoned stuffing mix, crushed
1 beaten egg
1 3 oz. can chopped mushrooms, drained (½ cup)
1/3 cup beef broth
¼ cup sliced green onion
¼ cup chopped almonds, toasted
¼ cup snipped parsley
1 teaspoon lemon juice
2 lb. ground beef
1 teaspoon salt

Nutritional Values:
Per Serving (excluding unknown items): 634 Calories; 52g Fat (73.7% calories from fat); 30g Protein; 12g Carbohydrate; 2g Dietary Fiber; 164mg Cholesterol; 815mg Sodium.
Points: 10

Substitute Values:
Per Serving (using substitute lean ground beef and whole wheat stuffing mix): 432 Calories; 7g Fat (46.7% calories from fat); 17g Protein; 2g Carbohydrate; trace Dietary Fiber; 52mg Cholesterol; 540mg Sodium.
Points: 9

Herbal Meat Loaf

Mix all ingredients and shape into loaf. Put in oiled bread pan. Bake at 325° about 60 min. for a moist loaf.

Servings: 6
Start to finish: 1:20 minutes

1 pound ground beef
1 cup shredded wheat®, biscuit
1 whole egg
1/4 teaspoon savory
2 teaspoons basil
1 tablespoon vegetable oil
1/2 teaspoon pepper
1/4 cup milk
1/4 cup red wine

Nutritional Values:
Per Serving (excluding unknown items): 300 Calories; 24g Fat (72.9% calories from fat); 15g Protein; 5g Carbohydrate; 1g Dietary Fiber; 101mg Cholesterol; 75mg Sodium.
Points: 8

Substitute Values:
Per Serving (using substitute lean roast, and 98% fat free mushroom soup): 243 Calories; 16g Fat (63.4% calories from fat); 16g Protein; 5g Carbohydrate; 1g Dietary Fiber; 89mg Cholesterol; 74mg Sodium.
Points: 6

Oriental Meatballs

Combine meat mixture and roll in bite size balls. Brown at 450° for 10 min. turning once.

Combine and heat sauce, simmer for 5 min. Add 2 tablespoons cornstarch mixed in water. Cook until thick. Pour over meatballs and serve as main dish or as canapes.

Servings: 4
Start to finish: 30 minutes

Meat Mixture:
1 1/4 pounds Ground beef
3/4 cup oats
1/2 cup milk
8 ounces water chestnut, canned
1 tablespoon Worcestershire sauce
1/2 teaspoon onion powder
1/2 teaspoon garlic powder
2 tablespoons soy sauce

Sauce:
1 cup sugar
3/4 cup vinegar
1/4 cup ketchup
1 teaspoon paprika
1/2 teaspoon salt
3 teaspoons soy sauce
1/2 teaspoon ginger
3/4 cup water

Nutritional Values:
Per Serving (excluding unknown items): 554 Calories; 27g Fat (43.7% calories from fat); 21g Protein; 58g Carbohydrate; 3g Dietary Fiber; 83mg Cholesterol; 915mg Sodium.
Points: 13

Substitute Values:
Per Serving (using lean ground beef and sugar substitute): 428 Calories; 4g Fat (13.1% calories from fat); 14g Protein; 39g Carbohydrate; 3g Dietary Fiber; 26mg Cholesterol; 942mg Sodium.
Points: 8

Short Ribs of Beef

Salt and pepper short ribs and roll in flour. Place in baking dish and bake at 350° about 2 hours. Combine ketchup, water, vinegar, Worcestershire sauce, soy sauce, sugar and onions. When ribs begin to brown baste with sauce.

Servings: 4
Start to finish: 2:30 minutes

3 pounds short ribs
3/4 cup ketchup
3/4 cup water, 2
2 tablespoons vinegar
2 tablespoons Worcestershire sauce
2 tablespoons soy sauce
1/2 cup sugar
2 whole onions, small, thinly sliced.

Nutritional Values:
Per Serving (excluding unknown items): 177 Calories; trace Fat (1.4% calories from fat); 2g Protein; 45g Carbohydrate; 2g Dietary Fiber; trace Cholesterol; 1125mg Sodium.
Points: 3

Substitute Values:
Per Serving (using sugar substitute and lean beef): 128 Calories; trace Fat (2.0% calories from fat); 2g Protein; 30g Carbohydrate; 2g Dietary Fiber; trace Cholesterol; 1173mg Sodium.
Points: 2

Bundle Burgers

Mix carnation milk with hamburger and make flat patties. Put a spoonful of dressing (cooked according to package) in middle of patty and make into meatball. Mix together mushroom soup, Worcestershire sauce, ketchup, and water. Place meatballs in baking dish and pour soup mixture over balls and bake in oven at 350° for 45 min.

Servings: 4
Start to finish: 60 minutes

5 ounces seasoned bread stuffing, pork
1 pound ground beef
1/4 cup evaporated milk
10 2/3 ounces mushroom soup golden, 1 can
1 tablespoon Worcestershire sauce
2 tablespoons ketchup
1/2 cup water or 1/2 soup can of water

Nutritional Values:
Per Serving (excluding unknown items): 514 Calories; 32g Fat (57.2% calories from fat); 25g Protein; 29g Carbohydrate; 2g Dietary Fiber; 102mg Cholesterol; 1161mg Sodium.
Points: 13

Substitute Values:
Per Serving (using substitute lean beef 95%, and skimmed evaporated milk): 439 Calories; 3g Fat (14.4% calories from fat); 17g Protein; 29g Carbohydrate; 2g Dietary Fiber; 32mg Cholesterol; 1119mg Sodium.
Points: 9

Lamb Chops with Mandarins

(New Zealand Style)

Brown and season chops with salt and pepper. Simmer in sauce pan for ½ hour wine and mandarin juice, then thicken juices with cornstarch and water. Add Mandarin pieces and cook one minute. Pour sauce over chops to serve.

Servings: 4
Start to finish: 60 minutes

6 lamb chop, lean
Salt and Pepper, to taste
1/2 cup mandarin orange juice, or orange
1 tablespoon butter, or more if needed
1/2 cup white wine
1/2 cup mandarin oranges, pieces
1 tablespoon cornstarch, or more if needed

Nutritional Values:
Per Serving (excluding unknown items): 519 Calories; 41g Fat (74.5% calories from fat); 24g Protein; 8g Carbohydrate; 1g Dietary Fiber; 113mg Cholesterol; 111mg Sodium.
Points: 14

Substitute Values:
Per Serving (using substitute lean lamb chops): 334 Calories; 14g Fat (40.1% calories from fat); 38g Protein; 8g Carbohydrate; 1g Dietary Fiber; 127mg Cholesterol; 154mg Sodium.
Points: 8

Lamb Meatballs with Lemon Sauce

Cook rice and onion in water and cover for 10 min. Drain and add ground lamb. Add white of egg (save yolk for sauce), chipped parsley, salt, pepper to taste. Mix well and shape into balls the size of a walnut. Cut cone out of cabbage and place in kettle of hot water just long enough to soften so leaves can be rolled without breaking. Drain and separate leaves. Place meat ball in cabbage leaf and roll, then place in cooking kettle in which a lump of butter has been melted. Add enough water to come to top of meatballs. Sprinkle with salt and pepper and cook slowly for 1 hour. When ready to serve, beat egg yolk and add juice of lemon slowly. Then drain liquid off meatballs and add egg and lemon to it, beating constantly. Pour this over the meatballs and keep hot., but don not boil again. Serve with salad and any kind of bread.

Servings: 4
Start to finish: 1:30 minutes

6 lamb chop
Salt and Pepper, to taste
1/2 cup mandarin orange juice, or orange
1 tablespoon butter, or more if needed
1/2 cup white wine
1/2 cup mandarin oranges, pieces
1 tablespoon cornstarch, or more if needed

Nutritional Values:
Per Serving (excluding unknown items): 519 Calories; 41g Fat (74.5% calories from fat); 24g Protein; 8g Carbohydrate; 1g Dietary Fiber; 113mg Cholesterol; 111mg Sodium.
Points: 14

Substitute Values:
Per Serving (using substitute lamb chop, lean): 334 Calories; 14g Fat (40.1% calories from fat); 38g Protein; 8g Carbohydrate; 1g Dietary Fiber; 127mg Cholesterol; 154mg Sodium.
Points: 8

Veal and Pork Kabobs

Put meat on sticks, dip in egg, wine and Ritz crackers crumbs. Brown in electric cooker or electric grill. Cook slowly until done.

Great Cold too!

Servings: 4
Start to finish: 30-40 minutes

2 pounds veal, cubed
2 pounds pork , cubed
1 whole egg, beaten
1/2 cup wine, red or white
1 1/2 cups crackers, Ritz

Nutritional Values:
Per Serving (excluding unknown items): 376 Calories; 13g Fat (34.1% calories from fat); 27g Protein; 32g Carbohydrate; 1g Dietary Fiber; 120mg Cholesterol; 689mg Sodium.
Points: 8

Substitute Values:
Per Serving (using substitute lean pork and veal): 212 Calories; 6g Fat (26.2% calories from fat); 5g Protein; 32g Carbohydrate; 1g Dietary Fiber; 27mg Cholesterol; 596mg Sodium.
Points: 5

Pakistani Shish Kabobs

Mix ground beef, dried chili, cumin, salt, pepper, curry powder, egg, flour and onion flakes together and shape into elongated meatballs and cook over charcoal. Serve with onion chutney by combing sliced onion, vinegar, mint leaves and water in a bowl. Use heated flour tortillas as a utensil instead of fork.

Servings: 6
Start to finish: 45 minutes

2 pounds ground
3 dried chilies , crumbled
1/2 teaspoon cumin
salt and pepper, to taste
1/2 teaspoon curry powder
1 whole egg
1 teaspoon flour
1 teaspoon onion flakes
1 whole onion, sliced
1 1/2 teaspoons vinegar
1 1/2 teaspoons mint leaves, crushed
2/3 cup water, to about cover

Nutritional Values:
Per Serving (excluding unknown items): 493 Calories; 41g Fat (76.1% calories from fat); 27g Protein; 2g Carbohydrate; trace Dietary Fiber; 164mg Cholesterol; 117mg Sodium.
Points: 13

Substitute Values:
Per Serving (using substitute ground beef, 95% lean): 405 Calories; 4g Fat (34.5% calories from fat); 16g Protein; 2g Carbohydrate; trace Dietary Fiber; 77mg Cholesterol; 58mg Sodium.
Points: 8

Indonesian Shish-Kabobs

Place meat alternating chicken, pork and veal on skewers. Brush with clarified butter, then brush with mixture of garlic, onion, ground coriander, curry powder, soy sauce, lemon, peanut butter, pepper and salt. Broil about 6 min. turning often and basting with mixture as you go. Serve with rice.

Servings: 4
Start to finish: 30 minutes

5 ounces chicken breast
5 ounces pork loin
5 ounces veal
1 clove garlic, smashed
1 whole onion, small sliced thin
2 teaspoons ground coriander
2 teaspoons curry powder
2 teaspoons soy sauce
1/4 cup lemon juice
1 cup peanut butter, creamy
salt and pepper, to taste

Nutritional Values:
Per Serving (excluding unknown items): 535 Calories; 39g Fat (63.1% calories from fat); 34g Protein; 18g Carbohydrate; 5g Dietary Fiber; 58mg Cholesterol; 531mg Sodium.
Points: 13

Substitute Values:
Per Serving (using substitute lean pork and veal): 535 Calories; 38g Fat (61.5% calories from fat); 36g Protein; 18g Carbohydrate; 5g Dietary Fiber; 64mg Cholesterol; 536mg Sodium.
Points: 13

Veal Parmesan

Saute onion and garlic in olive oil or butter until onion is limp. Add chopped tomatoes, sugar basil and cook slowly 15 min. stirring often. Add parsley and cook 10 min. longer.

Season meat liberally on both sides with salt and pepper. Heat olive oil in large skillet. Brown veal quickly on both sides; lift out. Top each cutlet with thin slices mozzarella, tomato sauce, and sprinkle top liberally with Parmesan cheese. Broil until cheese melts, bubbly and golden brown. Serve at once.

For Fresh Tomato Sauce:
1 whole onion, large
2 cloves garlic, peeled and crushed
1/4 cup extra virgin olive oil, or butter
4 whole tomatoes, peeled and chopped
1/2 teaspoon sugar
1 teaspoon dried basil
2 sprigs parsley, chopped

For Veal Cutlets:
1 1/2 pounds Veal cutlets
salt and pepper
1/4 cup extra virgin olive oil
3/4 pound mozzarella cheese
16 ounces tomato sauce
Parmesan cheese, freshly grated

Nutritional Values:
Per Serving (excluding unknown items): 841 Calories; 60g Fat (63.9% calories from fat); 55g Protein; 21g Carbohydrate; 5g Dietary Fiber; 216mg Cholesterol; 1208mg Sodium.
Points: 21

Substitute Values:
Per Serving (using substitute lean veal, fat-free mozzarella cheese and fat-free Parmesan cheese): 411 Calories; 24g Fat (50.0% calories from fat); 31g Protein; 22g Carbohydrate; 5g Dietary Fiber; 77mg Cholesterol; 1618mg Sodium.
Points: 9

Spare Ribs Soya

Flour and brown ribs, drain fat and mix lemon juice, garlic, soy sauce, and ginger. Pour over ribs. Bake in dutch oven at 350° for 1 ½ hours. Carrots may be put in with meat if desired.

Servings: 4
Start to finish: 30 minutes

3 pounds spareribs, country style
1/4 cup lemon juice
2 cloves garlic, crushed
1/2 cup soy sauce
1 tablespoon ground ginger
1/2 cup flour, to coat

Nutritional Values:
Per Serving (excluding unknown items): 690 Calories; 50g Fat (66.2% calories from fat); 40g Protein; 18g Carbohydrate; 1g Dietary Fiber; 165mg Cholesterol; 2219mg Sodium.
Points: 18

Substitute Values:
Per Serving (using lean meat substitute): 87 Calories; trace Fat (2.7% calories from fat); 4g Protein; 18g Carbohydrate; 1g Dietary Fiber; 0mg Cholesterol; 2059mg Sodium.
Points: 2

Oven Barbecue Spareribs

Cut meat into pieces suitable for serving and placed in roaster. Top with onion slices. Mix remaining ingredients and pour over ribs. Bake at 375° 1 ½ to 2 hours, basting occasionally.

Servings: 4
Start to finish: 2:30 minutes

4 pounds Spareribs
2 whole onion, sliced
2 tablespoons vinegar
2 tablespoons Worcestershire sauce
1 teaspoon salt, 1/2" cubes
1/8 teaspoon pepper
1/2 teaspoon chili powder
3/4 cup ketchup
3/4 cup water

Nutritional Values:
Per Serving (excluding unknown items): 587 Calories; 44g Fat (68.6% calories from fat); 33g Protein; 13g Carbohydrate; 1g Dietary Fiber; 146mg Cholesterol; 907mg Sodium.
Points: 15

Substitute Values:
Per Serving (using substitute beef lean spareribs): 51 Calories; trace Fat (3.1% calories from fat); 1g Protein; 13g Carbohydrate; 1g Dietary Fiber; 0mg Cholesterol; 764mg Sodium.
Points: 2

Pineapple Spareribs

Mix pineapple preserves, orange juice, lemon juice, soy sauce, ginger, rosemary, pepper and garlic. Place spareribs in shallow dish and let stand for 3-4 hours or longer refrigerated. Turning occasionally. Remove spareribs and place on a rack in an open roasting pan. Do not add water. Do not cover. Roast in a moderate oven 350° to 2 to 2 ½ hours, basting with marinade every half hour.

Servings: 8
Start to finish: 2:30 minutes

6 pounds spareribs
3/4 cup pineapple preserves
1/2 cup orange juice
1 tablespoon lemon juice
1/2 cup soy sauce
1 teaspoon ginger
1/4 teaspoon rosemary
1/4 teaspoon pepper
1 clove garlic, minced

Nutritional Values:
Per Serving (excluding unknown items): 622 Calories; 50g Fat (73.3% calories from fat); 37g Protein; 4g Carbohydrate; trace Dietary Fiber; 165mg Cholesterol; 1189mg Sodium.
Points: 17

Substitute Values:
Per Serving (using substitute beef flank or other lean meat): 19 Calories; trace Fat (3.1% calories from fat); 1g Protein; 4g Carbohydrate; trace Dietary Fiber; 0mg Cholesterol; 1029mg Sodium.
Points: 1

Stuffed Green Peppers

6 whole Green Peppers
1 pound ground pork, cooked
1/2 cup rice, cooked al dente'
1 1/2 cups water
2 tablespoons onion, chopped

Parboil (cook partially by boiling for a brief period) green peppers.
for 5 min. Cool. Combine in mixing bowl cooked sausage, rice, water and onion. Stuff peppers with rice sausage mixture and bake at 350° for 20 to 30 min.

Servings: 6
Start to finish: 50 minutes

Nutritional Values:
Per Serving (excluding unknown items): 405 Calories; 31g Fat (68.4% calories from fat); 11g Protein; 21g Carbohydrate; 2g Dietary Fiber; 51mg Cholesterol; 510mg Sodium.
Points: 10

Substitute Values:
Per Serving (using substitute lean pork sausage): 90 Calories; trace Fat (3.2% calories from fat); 2g Protein; 20g Carbohydrate; 2g Dietary Fiber; 0mg Cholesterol; 5mg Sodium.
Points: 1

Super Curry

Place meat in large casserole and sprinkle with coconut, almonds and onion. Drizzle syrup over this. Mix curry powder with soup and pour over top. Cover and bake in a slow oven 300° for 3 ½ hours (if meat is pre-cooked, 2 hours, is enough).

Servings: 4
Start to finish: 3:30 minutes

3 pounds veal, or lamb cut up
1/2 cup shredded coconut meat
1/2 cup almonds, slivered
1 whole onion, chopped
1/4 cup Karo syrup
5 teaspoons curry powder
10 1/2 ounces cream of chicken soup, no water

Nutritional Values:
Per Serving (excluding unknown items): 743 Calories; 38g Fat (46.5% calories from fat); 71g Protein; 28g Carbohydrate; 4g Dietary Fiber; 282mg Cholesterol; 611mg Sodium.
Points: 17

Substitute Values:
Per Serving (using substitute lean veal or lamb): 252 Calories; 15g Fat (50.9% calories from fat); 6g Protein; 28g Carbohydrate; 4g Dietary Fiber; 3mg Cholesterol; 332mg Sodium.
Points: 5

Sweet and Sour Pork

Brown pork in a small amount of oil in skillet, add tomato juice and bring to boil. Cover pineapple, reserving syrup. Combine sugar and cornstarch, add syrup from pineapple, vinegar and add to pork, stirring until thickened. Add pineapple , green pepper, and onion and cook 3 minutes longer. Serve over hot fluffy rice.

Servings: 4
Start to finish: 30 minutes

1/2 pound pork shoulder , cut in 2" strips, ½ wide
8 ounces pineapple chunks , tidbits
2 tablespoons brown sugar
2 tablespoons vinegar
1 tablespoon cornstarch
1 cup tomato juice, low sodium
1 whole green pepper, small, cut into strips
1/4 cup onion, cut into strips

Nutritional Values:
Per Serving (excluding unknown items): 182 Calories; 8g Fat (37.5% calories from fat); 8g Protein; 21g Carbohydrate; 2g Dietary Fiber; 30mg Cholesterol; 251mg Sodium.
Points: 4

Substitute Values:
Per Serving (using substitute pork shoulder lean and pineapple chunks in light syrup): 77 Calories; trace Fat (1.9% calories from fat); 1g Protein; 20g Carbohydrate; 2g Dietary Fiber; 0mg Cholesterol; 10mg Sodium.
Points: 1

Barbecued Wieners

Split wiener (12) in half and place in baking dish. Combine ingredients and pour over wieners. Cook in oven at 350° for 30 min.

Servings: 6
Start to finish: 40 minutes

12 Hot Dogs Weiner's
1 whole onion, chopped
3 tablespoons oil, brown onion in
1 tablespoon sugar
1 teaspoon dry mustard
salt and pepper, to taste
1/2 cup ketchup
1/2 cup water
1/4 cup vinegar
1 tablespoon Worcestershire sauce
1 drop Tabasco sauce

Nutritional Values:
Per Serving (excluding unknown items): 465 Calories; 40g Fat (77.3% calories from fat); 13g Protein; 13g Carbohydrate; 1g Dietary Fiber; 57mg Cholesterol; 1540mg Sodium.
Points: 12

Substitute Values:
Per Serving (using substitute Hebrew National 97% Fat Free): 191 Calories; 10g Fat (67.4% calories from fat); 1g Protein; 10g Carbohydrate; 1g Dietary Fiber; 30mg Cholesterol; 1063mg Sodium.
Points: 4

Sarma

This dish takes some time but well worth it!

Boil ham hock in water in covered pan. Quickly boil head of cabbage to make leaves soft (bring water to boiling point then turn off heat, letting cabbage remain in hot water for ½). In the meantime , chop ham and saute with onion, and ground round. Remove from heat and add uncooked rice and raw egg. Season lightly with salt. Set aside. Remove husk from boiled cabbage so that each leaf is easy to roll. Rinse leaf with hot water if brittle. Cover bottom of big pot with small leaves so that Sarma won't burn while cooking. Take each leaf and fill with rice, ham, ground round mixture, and roll (jelly roll style). Tuck in ends and stack in big pot. Toss in sauerkraut, polish sausage and ham hocks (with water). Cover and simmer at least 2 hours.

Super good served with boiled potatoes, a cold Beer, and French bread.

Servings: 8
Start to finish: 2:30 minutes

1 pound ground round
1 pound ham
1 whole onion, chopped
1 whole egg
1 head cabbage
32 ounces sauerkraut
1/2 pound ham shank, boned
2 whole polish sausage
1/4 cup rice
1 clove garlic
bacon grease , for sauting
salt

Nutritional Values:
Per Serving (excluding unknown items): 482 Calories; 33g Fat (62.0% calories from fat); 31g Protein; 14g Carbohydrate; 3g Dietary Fiber; 138mg Cholesterol; 2043mg Sodium.
Points: 12

Substitute Values:
Per Serving (using substitute lean ham and lean ground beef): 245 Calories; 17g Fat (62.7% calories from fat); 11g Protein; 12g Carbohydrate; 3g Dietary Fiber; 66mg Cholesterol; 1258mg Sodium.
Points: 6

Salsa Sauce

Mix all together and simmer 1 hour. Serve at room temperature. Good with hamburgers, tacos, scrambled eggs, etc..

Servings: 4
Start to finish: 1:10 minutes

1 can stewed tomatoes cut up
1 4oz. can dried chilies
1 bunch green onions, sliced thin, tops and all
1 teaspoon salt
½ teaspoon pepper
1 tablespoon sugar

Nutritional Values:
Per Serving (excluding unknown items): 212 Calories; 1g Fat (3.0% calories from fat); 6g Protein; 52g Carbohydrate; 8g Dietary Fiber; 0mg Cholesterol; 3579mg Sodium.
Points: 4

Mushroom Gravy

In saucepan bring to boil all ingredients, then reduce heat to medium.

Add sliced mushrooms(fresh), juice of 1 lemon, 1 T or more cornstarch, (Dissolve cornstarch in ½ glass of water), 1 or more T kitchen Bouquet until desired color (light to dark brown).

Boil slowly until desired thickness. If too thick cut with wine.

Servings: 6
Start to finish: 30 minutes

16 ounces water
1 3/4 ounces olive oil
1 tablespoon salt
1 teaspoon herbs, fine
1 1/2 teaspoons garlic salt, or 1 clove garlic minced
1 tablespoon MSG (optional)
16 ounces red wine
2 tablespoons instant onions, minced
1 teaspoon coarse pepper
1 teaspoon marjoram
1 teaspoon oregano
1 1/2 teaspoons Worcestershire sauce
2 cups mushrooms, fresh sliced
juice of 1 lemon
cornstarch (dissolved in water) to thicken
kitchen bouquet for color

Nutritional Values:
Per Serving (excluding unknown items): 137 Calories; 8g Fat (83.3% calories from fat); 1g Protein; 3g Carbohydrate; 1g Dietary Fiber; 0mg Cholesterol; 1943mg Sodium.
Points: 3

Substitute Values:
Per Serving (using substitute imitation margarine and ½ the wine): 65 Calories; 3g Fat (70.4% calories from fat); 1g Protein; 2g Carbohydrate; 1g Dietary Fiber; 0mg Cholesterol; 1998mg Sodium.
Points: 1

Teriyaki Marinade

Mix well. Excellent for flank steak. Marinade about 6 hours. May be kept in refrigerator.

6 hours to marinate

1/2 cup soy sauce
3 tablespoons honey
2 tablespoons vinegar
1 1/2 teaspoons ginger, chopped
1 1/2 teaspoons garlic, minced
2 whole green onion, cut small
3/4 cup extra virgin olive oil, vegetable or olive

Nutritional Values:
Per Serving (excluding unknown items): 218 Calories; 20g Fat (82.1% calories from fat); 1g Protein; 9g Carbohydrate; trace Dietary Fiber; 0mg Cholesterol; 1030mg Sodium.
Points: 6

Substitute Values:
Per Serving (using substitute Enova oil and low sodium soy sauce): 38 Calories; trace Fat (3.4% calories from fat); 1g Protein; 9g Carbohydrate; trace Dietary Fiber; 0mg Cholesterol; 601mg Sodium.
Points: 1

NOTES:

POULTRY AND SEAFOOD

POULTRY AND SEAFOOD

Grandma's Lemon Chicken

Pound Chicken breast flat. Heat frying pan with oil and butter. Lightly flour chicken breast. Place chicken in pan and saute about 3-4 min on each side, (remember your sauteing, not frying). Then add to pan ginger, lemon zest, garlic, salt and pepper when you flip to the second side. Remove from pan and place in warming plate in oven while finishing up.

Turn up the heat on the pan and de-glaze with wine, chicken stock, and lemon juice; add scallion and or mushrooms (optional). Boil and reduced to half. Add the parsley and return the chicken and any accumulated juices to the pan for reheating. Heat through and then serve immediately.

Servings: 6
Start to finish: 30-40 minutes

4 chicken breasts, boneless, skinless
1/2 cup lemon juice, freshly ground
1/2 teaspoon lemon zest
1 1/2 cloves garlic, minced
2 tablespoons ginger, minced
1/4 cup parsley, chopped
1/2 cup chicken stock
1/2 cup white wine
1 tablespoon olive oil
1 tablespoon butter
1/4 cup Flour, to coat chicken
3 whole scallions, chopped
1 cup mushrooms, sliced

Nutritional Values:
Per Serving (excluding unknown items): 275 Calories; 9g Fat (29.8% calories from fat); 36g Protein; 9g Carbohydrate; 1g Dietary Fiber; 101mg Cholesterol; 287mg Sodium.
Points: 6

Substitute Values:
Per Serving (using substitute using fat free chicken stock, no olive oil and half the flour to coat): 245 Calories; 6g Fat (24.6% calories from fat); 36g Protein; 7g Carbohydrate; 1g Dietary Fiber; 101mg Cholesterol; 145mg Sodium.
Points: 5

Oven Fried Chicken in Herb Gravy

Arrange pieces skin side down in one layer in buttered shallow baking dish. Sprinkle with onion. Pour melted butter with poultry seasoning and spoon a little over each piece. Bake uncovered at 350° (moderate oven) 1 to 1 ¼ hours until tender and lightly browned. After first half hour turn and baste with more butter.

Just before serving, pour mushroom soup diluted with milk around chicken and bake another 30-30 min. Serve chicken with gravy spooned over.

Servings: 4
Start to finish: 1 to 1 ½ hours

1 whole chicken
1/2 cup onion, chopped
1/4 cup butter
10.75 ounces cream of mushroom soup, diluted with milk
poultry seasoning

Nutritional Values:
Per Serving (excluding unknown items): 660 Calories; 55g Fat (75.3% calories from fat); 36g Protein; 4g Carbohydrate; trace Dietary Fiber; 173mg Cholesterol; 559mg Sodium.
Points: 18

Substitute Values:
Per Serving (using substitute chicken dark meat, no skin, cream of mushroom soup fat free, and imitation margarine): 58 Calories; 6g Fat (85.9% calories from fat); trace Protein; 2g Carbohydrate; trace Dietary Fiber; trace Cholesterol; 142mg Sodium.
Points: 2

Chicken Divan

Heat chicken soup and add mayonnaise, lemon juice, curry powder, and cheese. Add bread crumbs to melted butter. Arrange chicken breasts over broccoli in casserole. Pour soup mixture over all. Place buttered crumbs on top. Bake at 350° 25 to 30 min.

Servings: 8
Start to finish: 30 minutes

4 chicken breast, boiled
24 ounces broccoli, frozen, cooked
21 1/2 ounces cream of chicken soup
1 cup mayonnaise
1 tablespoon lemon juice
1/2 teaspoon curry powder
1/2 cup sharp cheddar cheese
1/2 cup bread crumbs
1 tablespoon butter, melted

Nutritional Values:
Per Serving (excluding unknown items): 765 Calories; 58g Fat (66.7% calories from fat); 49g Protein; 16g Carbohydrate; 4g Dietary Fiber; 156mg Cholesterol; 924mg Sodium.
Points: 19

Substitute Values:
Per Serving (using substitute cream of chicken 98% fat free, fat-free mayonnaise, fat-free cheddar cheese, whole wheat bread crumbs, and imitation margarine): 339 Calories; 15g Fat (39.4% calories from fat); 36g Protein; 15g Carbohydrate; 3g Dietary Fiber; 94mg Cholesterol; 616mg Sodium.
Points: 7

Chicken Loaves

Boil 2-3 lb. Chicken in salted water with minced onion, celery and parsley., until done (about 45min). Remove from broth – cool, strain broth and reserve.

Remove meat from bones. Cut up chicken in small chunks. Melt 2 T margarine in 2 C hot milk. Mix with chicken 2 C soft stale bread crumbs, ¼ tsp pepper, 1 tsp salt, accent, ¼ C celery, 2 T green peppers minced, 2 T diced pimento, and 4 beaten eggs. Put in well greased loaf pan (9"x5"x3"). Bake at 350° 1 hour.

Serve hot loaf with curry sauce. For curry sauce add 1 tsp (I like more) curry powder to 1 10oz. Can or jar chicken gravy and heat. Turn hot loaf out on warm serving platter. Cover with sauce. Add paprika and serve. Asparagus with lemon butter is great with this.

Servings: 8
Start to finish: 2:30 minutes

3 pounds chicken breast without skin
1/4 teaspoon pepper
2 cups milk, hot
3/4 cup onion, chopped
3/4 cup celery, chopped
3/4 cup parsley, chopped
1 teaspoon salt
1 teaspoon accent® seasoning mix (optional)
1/4 cup parsley
2 tablespoons pimento, diced
1 teaspoon curry powder, or more if needed
10 ounces chicken gravy mix, jar or can
paprika
2 cups whole wheat bread crumbs
1/4 teaspoon pepper
1/4 teaspoon salt
1/4 cup celery
2 tablespoons green peppers, minced
2 tablespoons pimento, deiced
4 whole eggs, beaten

Nutritional Values:
Per Serving Size (excluding unknown items): 462 Calories; 8g Fat (16.4% calories from fat); 41g Protein; 49g Carbohydrate; 2g Dietary Fiber; 193mg Cholesterol; 2761mg Sodium.
Points: 6

Substitute Values:
Per Serving (using substitute Egg Beaters® 99% egg substitute, whole wheat bread crumbs): 446 Calories; 6g Fat (12.1% calories from fat); 43g Protein; 49g Carbohydrate; 4g Dietary Fiber; 87mg Cholesterol; 2800mg Sodium.
Points: 6

Mom's Honey Chicken

Melt margarine in sauce pan and add rest of ingredients to mixture. Pour over chicken pieces that have been salted and peppered. Bake at 350° for 1 hour, turning once.

Servings: 4
Start to finish: 1:10 minutes

4 chicken breasts halves boneless, skinless
1/4 margarine – melt in pan
1 cup honey
1 T tablespoon ginger minced and crushed
1 tablespoon lemon juice
2 tablespoon soy sauce
1 teaspoon paprika

Nutritional Values:
Per Serving (excluding unknown items): 308 Calories; 13g Fat (37.8% calories from fat); 28g Protein; 20g Carbohydrate; trace Dietary Fiber; 68mg Cholesterol; 726mg Sodium.
Points: 7

Substitute Values:
Per Serving (using substitute imitation margarine): 256 Calories; 7g Fat (25.4% calories from fat); 28g Protein; 20g Carbohydrate; trace Dietary Fiber; 68mg Cholesterol; 732mg Sodium.
Points: 6

Fried Chicken

Cut and rinse Chicken do not pat dry. Generously pour flour into large mixing bowl. Generously add salt, pepper and garlic salt to flour and mix. Generously salt and pepper chicken and roll around in flour mixture. After all pieces have been floured place in heated shortening. For chicken with bones fry turning every 5 min. until golden brown. Always check chicken with meat thermometer. Boneless chicken until golden brown. Place chicken pieces on paper towels to soak up excess oil.

Servings: 4
Start to finish: 30 minutes

Note:
It's always best to use a shortening if your frying and your recipe calls for it. Shortening makes baked and fried goods fluffier and flakier, while oils provide a denser and heavier texture

1 Whole Chicken or 4 Boneless Chicken Breasts halves
1 to 2 cups Flour
salt and Pepper
Garlic salt
Crisco Shortening sticks (3pk)

Nutritional Values:
Per Serving (excluding unknown items): 1488 Calories; 132g Fat (79.7% calories from fat); 51g Protein; 24g Carbohydrate; 1g Dietary Fiber; 235mg Cholesterol; 184mg Sodium.
Points: 41

Substitute Values:
Per Serving (using substitute chicken breasts no bone no skin and Enova cooking oil): 246 Calories; 2g Fat (7.7% calories from fat); 30g Protein; 24g Carbohydrate; 1g Dietary Fiber; 68mg Cholesterol; 77mg Sodium.
Points: 5

Baked Chicken with Wine

4 chicken breast halves, skinless
10 3/4 ounces mushroom soup, no water
1/2 cup white wine
1 envelope onion soup mix
4 ounces mushrooms, canned (optional)

Mix mushroom soup, wine, water, and onion soup mix. Pour over chicken pieces that have been placed in a baking dish. Cover and bake 350° for about 1 hour 15 min. Pour sauce over chicken.

Servings: 4
Start to finish: 1:30 minutes

Nutritional Values:
Per Serving (excluding unknown items): 185 Calories; 2g Fat (11.8% calories from fat); 29g Protein; 7g Carbohydrate; 2g Dietary Fiber; 69mg Cholesterol; 1074mg Sodium.
Points: 3

Substitute Values:
Per Serving (using substitute 98% Fat Free Cream of Mushroom Soup): 185 Calories; 2g Fat (11.8% calories from fat); 29g Protein; 7g Carbohydrate; 2g Dietary Fiber; 69mg Cholesterol; 1074mg Sodium.
Points: 3

Chicken ala Ogden

Saute mushrooms and onions in 1 T butter. Add 1 C white wine. Cook (simmer) about 10 min. Remove from heat, add 1 can cream mushroom soup, cheddar cheese. Mix and pour over chicken. Bake 1 hour at 325°.

Servings: 4
Start to finish: 1:20 minutes

3 cups mushroom pieces, sliced
1 whole onion, large sliced up
1 cup white wine
1 whole chicken, cut up or 4 chicken breasts halves
10 3/4 ounces cream of mushroom soup
1 cup grated cheddar cheese

Nutritional Values:
Per Serving (excluding unknown items): 801 Calories; 54g Fat (64.8% calories from fat); 57g Protein; 9g Carbohydrate; 1g Dietary Fiber; 266mg Cholesterol; 720mg Sodium.
Points: 20

Substitute Values:
Per Serving (using substitute boneless skinless chicken breasts, fat-free mushroom soup and fat free cheddar cheese): 260 Calories; 5g Fat (18.9% calories from fat); 38g Protein; 6g Carbohydrate; 1g Dietary Fiber; 74mg Cholesterol; 320mg Sodium.
Points: 5

Cheddar Chicken

Brown Chicken in butter. Saute' onion and pepper until tender. Put artichokes, chicken onion and peppers in casserole dish 9"x13". Put cheddar cheese soup and wine on top. Bake at 350° about 1 hour hour or until tender. Serve with rice.

Servings: 4-6
Start to finish: 1:20 minutes

4 chicken breast halves, skinless
cut in half
1/2 cup onion, chopped
1/2 cup green pepper, chopped
10 ounces artichoke hearts, jar
10 3/4 ounces cheddar cheese soup,
no water
1/2 cup white wine
2 tablespoons butter

Nutritional Values:
Per Serving (excluding unknown items): 166 Calories; 5g Fat (28.7% calories from fat); 20g Protein; 7g Carbohydrate; 3g Dietary Fiber; 56mg Cholesterol; 137mg Sodium.
Points: 3
Substitute Values:
Per Serving (using substitute imitation margarine): 149 Calories; 3g Fat (19.6% calories from fat); 20g Protein; 7g Carbohydrate; 3g Dietary Fiber; 46mg Cholesterol; 144mg Sodium.
Points: 3

Moroccan Tajeen
(Chicken with lemons and Green Olives)

Put in deep pan: onion garlic, parsley, pepper, and saffron. Put the chicken on this bed of spices, add enough water to reach half the height of the chicken, then put salt, mixed with coriander. Put a cover on the pan and allow water to start boiling, then add oil. From time to time turn over chicken; when the flesh is soft and the bones can be separated from flesh, take the chicken out and let sauce reduce until all the water is evaporated. Put the chicken back in deep pan, add the olives and lemon quartered. Let cook a few minutes. Serve hot on a deep plate with olives, lemons and then pour sauce from pan over all. Great with rice.

Servings: 4
Start to finish: 3:30 minutes
3 hours prep time (1 ½ if you use fryers)

1 whole chicken
1 whole onion, thinly sliced
1 clove garlic, chopped
1/4 cup parsley, chopped
1 tablespoon coriander seed,
not ground
1/2 teaspoon saffron
1/2 teaspoon ground pepper
3 tablespoons butter or margarine
10 ounces Spanish olives, Not stuffed
2 whole lemon

Nutritional Values:
Per Serving (excluding unknown items): 113 Calories; 11g Fat (75.0% calories from fat); 1g Protein; 7g Carbohydrate; 1g Dietary Fiber; 0mg Cholesterol; 5mg Sodium.
Points: 3

Substitute Values:
Per Serving (using substitute olive oil for imitation margarine): 61 Calories; 5g Fat (56.5% calories from fat); 1g Protein; 7g Carbohydrate; 1g Dietary Fiber; 0mg Cholesterol; 109mg Sodium.
Points: 1

Chicken Hawaii

Place chicken, water, onion salt, celery top in heavy kettle; cover and simmer gently 1 ½ to 2 hours or until tender. Allow chicken to cool in broth. Remove skin, then meat from bones; cut meat into bite-pieces. Return bones to broth and simmer 20 minutes; strain. Meanwhile, gently saute the chopped onion and celery in the butter or margarine until tender and transparent. Combine the salt, curry powder and flour; blend into onion celery mixture. Slowly stir in the strained chicken broth and cream; continue stirring until thickened. Simmer gently 10 minutes; add the chicken meat and sherry and keep warm. Cook the rice, following package directions. Halve the pineapples, leaving on the fronds. Remove the hard center core; score the pineapple meat. Fill the pineapple shell with rice and chicken mixture. Wrap pineapple in foil, being sure to cover the fronds. Place on the baking sheet and bake at 350° for 40 minutes. To serve, remove foil and garnish with chutney.

Servings: 8
Start to finish: 4 hours

4 pounds chicken breast half without skin, or whole stewing chicken
4 cups water
1 teaspoon onion salt
2 celery, tops
1/2 cup butter
1/2 teaspoon salt
1 tablespoon curry powder
1/2 cup flour
2 cups chicken broth
1 cup half-and-half
2 tablespoons sherry
3 cups rice , uncooked
3 whole pineapples, small
chutney, for garnish

Nutritional Values:
Per Serving (excluding unknown items): 436 Calories; 15g Fat (31.3% calories from fat); 45g Protein; 29g Carbohydrate; 3g Dietary Fiber; 136mg Cholesterol; 774mg Sodium.
Points: 9

Substitute Values:
Per Serving (using substitute boiled boned chicken breasts, fat free chicken broth, fat free half and half and imitation margarine): 399 Calories; 9g Fat (20.1% calories from fat); 46g Protein; 33g Carbohydrate; 3g Dietary Fiber; 105mg Cholesterol; 760mg Sodium.
Points: 8

Sweet and Sour Chicken

Sprinkle 2 ½ lb. Chicken pieces or parts with garlic salt. Let sit 45 min. refrigerated. Next Dip chicken in egg, then flour – back in egg, then flour and repeat one more time. Mix sauce and pour over chicken. Bake 45 min. to 1 hour in 325° - 350° oven.

Servings: 6
Start to finish: 1:45 minutes

2 1/2 pounds chicken breast pieces or chicken parts
2 eggs beaten
1 cup flour to coat

Sauce:
3/4 cup sugar
1/2 cup vinegar
3/4 tablespoon ketchup
1 teaspoon soy sauce
4 ounces pineapple , crushed or 1 small can

Nutritional Values:
Per Serving (excluding unknown items): 481 Calories; 21g Fat (40.1% calories from fat); 28g Protein; 43g Carbohydrate; 1g Dietary Fiber; 188mg Cholesterol; 195mg Sodium.
Points: 11

Substitute Values:
Per Serving (using substitute): 320 Calories; 4g Fat (11.0% calories from fat); 39g Protein; 29g Carbohydrate; 1g Dietary Fiber; 158mg Cholesterol; 250mg Sodium.
Points: 7

Pakistani Chicken Teeka

Remove skin from chicken pieces and score meat by making diagonal cuts in fat . Sprinkle with spices. Let stand, covered, in refrigerator for 1 hour, then sprinkle with juice of ½ lemon and charcoal. This dish must be charcoaled to be good and if your spices are fresh only use half the amount of the cumin and chilies the first time out.

Servings: 4
Start to finish: 1:30 minutes

4 chicken breasts with skin,
cut 1" thick cubes
2 teaspoons cumin
2 teaspoons chilies, red, drained and crumbled
1/4 teaspoon ginger
salt and pepper
1 lemon
1/4 teaspoon cardamom, optional

Nutritional Values:
Per Serving (excluding unknown items): 503 Calories; 27g Fat (49.9% calories from fat); 61g Protein; 1g Carbohydrate; trace Dietary Fiber; 186mg Cholesterol; 184mg Sodium.
Points: 12

Substitute Values:
Per Serving (using substitute chicken breast half without skin): 134 Calories; 2g Fat (12.0% calories from fat); 27g Protein; 1g Carbohydrate; trace Dietary Fiber; 68mg Cholesterol; 78mg Sodium.
Points: 3

Crisp Crusted Sole

Place sole in salt water for 5 min. Drain. Dip into egg, then into crumbs. Heat equal parts of oil and butter ¼ in. deep in frying pan. Add sole and brown quickly. Serve with lemon slices.

Servings: 4
Start to finish: 30 minutes

4 sole fillets
4 cups water
1 whole egg, beaten
1 cup cornflake crumbs
1 teaspoon salt
1 whole lemon, slices

Nutritional Values:
Per Serving (excluding unknown items): 250 Calories; 3g Fat (12.2% calories from fat); 34g Protein; 21g Carbohydrate; 1g Dietary Fiber; 131mg Cholesterol; 924mg Sodium.
Points: 5

Substitute Values:
Per Serving (using substitute bran flake crumbs): 170 Calories; 3g Fat (17.5% calories from fat); 32g Protein; 2g Carbohydrate; trace Dietary Fiber; 131mg Cholesterol; 690mg Sodium.
Points: 3

Chicken Juniper

Rub chicken with sherry and then honey.
Dust with flour and brown in butter.
Arrange in buttered baking dish; add gin and
sprinkle with parsley, onions and tarragon.
Bake at 350° for 1 hour. Remove chicken.
Blend arrowroot with ½ C liquid – return to
pan. Add cream; cook, stirring until
thickened. Salt to taste. Serve sauce over
chicken and sprinkle liberally with sesame
seeds.

Servings: 5
Start to finish: 1:20 minutes

2 pounds Chicken Breast, cut up
1/2 cup dry sherry
1/2 cup honey
1/2 cup flour
1/2 cup butter
1 1/2 cups gin
1/2 cup parsley
1/2 cup onion, chopped
1/2 teaspoon tarragon
2 tablespoons arrowroot
1 cup cream
salt, to taste
sesame seeds, to garnish

Nutritional Values:
Per Serving (excluding unknown items): 900
Calories; 44g Fat (55.9% calories from fat);
34g Protein; 44g Carbohydrate; 1g Dietary
Fiber; 135mg Cholesterol; 332mg Sodium.
Points: 21

Substitute Values:
Per Serving (using substitute fat free cream
and reduce alcohol): 675 Calories; 23g Fat
(39.0% calories from fat); 32g Protein; 47g
Carbohydrate; 1g Dietary Fiber; 93mg
Cholesterol; 371mg Sodium.
Points: 15

Pollo Flauta

(Little Flutes)

In saucepan, melt butter; blend in flour and salt. Add chicken broth. Cook and stir till mixture thickens and bubbles. Add lemon juice, parsley, onion, paprika, nutmeg and pepper. Stir in chicken. Cool slightly. Heat Oil. Soften tortilla first by dipping into heated oil only enough to soften. Makes them easier to roll.. Place about 1 T chicken mixture on tortilla. Roll up very tightly, securing with wooden toothpick. Fry in deep hot oil for 1-2 min. or until tortilla is crisp. Serve with avocado or guacamole.
Avocado Mix:
Mix 2 avocados in a bowl mashed., stir in ½ C sour cream, 1 T lime juice, ¼ tsp onion salt and about 10 drops hot sauce (optional).

Servings: 10-12
Start to finish: 45 minutes

3 tablespoons butter
1/4 cup flour, all purpose
1/4 teaspoon salt
1 cup chicken broth
1 tablespoon parsley, snipped
1 teaspoon onion, grated
1 dash paprika
1 dash ground nutmeg
1 dash pepper
1 1/2 cups chicken, cooked and diced
1 tablespoon lemon juice
24 corn tortillas
2 whole avocado, mashed
1/2 cup sour cream
1 tablespoon lime juice
1/4 teaspoon onion salt
hot sauce, optional
2 cups Crisco shortening,
or 3 pk sticks for frying

Nutritional Values:
Per Serving (excluding unknown items): 619 Calories; 54g Fat (76.8% calories from fat); 8g Protein; 29g Carbohydrate; 4g Dietary Fiber; 31mg Cholesterol; 275mg Sodium.
Points: 16

Substitute Values:
Per Serving (2 flutes) (using substitute Enova cooking oil, fat free sour cream and imitation margarine): 243 Calories; 11g Fat (39.7% calories from fat); 9g Protein; 29g Carbohydrate; 4g Dietary Fiber; 20mg Cholesterol; 260mg Sodium.
Points: 5

Shrimp Fillets of Sole Rolls

Saute lightly in butter onion, shrimp and mushroom. Spread mixture over fillets. Roll up and fasten with toothpicks. Place in large shallow buttered dish or pan. Mix soup and wine, pour over fillets, sprinkle a little paprika, then cheese. Bake until fish flakes off when pierced with a fork.

Servings: 6
Start to finish: 60 minutes

6 sole fillets, large fillets
1 cup onion, small chopped
1 cup shrimp, cooked
40 ounces mushrooms, canned, sliced
10 1/2 ounces -
cream of mushroom soup
1/2 cup white wine
1/2 cup cheddar cheese, shredded
1 1/2 tablespoons margarine or butter

Nutritional Values:
Per Serving (excluding unknown items): 349 Calories; 11g Fat (29.3% calories from fat); 45g Protein; 14g Carbohydrate; 5g Dietary Fiber; 156mg Cholesterol; 1293mg Sodium.
Points: 7

Substitute Values:
Per Serving (using substitute fat free cheddar and fat free cream of mushroom soup): 285 Calories; 5g Fat (14.9% calories from fat); 45g Protein; 12g Carbohydrate; 5g Dietary Fiber; 140mg Cholesterol; 1099mg Sodium.
Points: 5

Lemon Shrimp

Saute in garlic butter. Add tomato sauce, water and lemon juice. Simmer 15 min. Add shrimp and cook 5 min. or until pink and tender. Don't over cook. Serve as main course over rice which has been cooked in water with bouillon cube added.

Servings: 4
Start to finish: 30 minutes

1/4 cup butter
1 clove garlic, diced
1 small can tomato sauce
1 small can water
1/2 cup lemon juice
1 lb. Medium size prawns,
shelled and veined

Nutritional Values:
Per Serving (excluding unknown items): 34 Calories; 3g Fat (67.8% calories from fat); trace Protein; 3g Carbohydrate; trace Dietary Fiber; 8mg Cholesterol; 30mg Sodium.
Points: 1

Substitute Values:
Per Serving (using substitute imitation margarine): 21 Calories; 1g Fat (50.8% calories from fat); trace Protein; 3g Carbohydrate; trace Dietary Fiber; 0mg Cholesterol; 35mg Sodium.
Points: 1

Mexican Prawns and Pineapple

Melt butter in skillet over medium heat. Add prawn, pepper, and pineapple. Season generously, salt, pepper and chili powder. Saute' shrimp till pink and green pepper is tender crisp. 8-10 min. Serve over buttered rice. Garnish with lots of fresh lime wedges. Squeeze lime over as you eat.

Servings: 4
Start to finish: 20 minutes

3 tablespoons butter
1 pound prawns, shells removed and veined
1 small green pepper, seeded and cut into rings
salt and pepper, to taste
2 teaspoons chili powder, to taste
3 cups pineapple, cut in chunks

Nutritional Values:
Per Serving (excluding unknown items): 145 Calories; 9g Fat (54.1% calories from fat); 1g Protein; 17g Carbohydrate; 2g Dietary Fiber; 23mg Cholesterol; 102mg Sodium.
Points: 3

Substitute Values:
Per Serving (using substitute 2 T imitation margarine): 94 Calories; 4g Fat (31.0% calories from fat); 1g Protein; 17g Carbohydrate; 2g Dietary Fiber; 0mg Cholesterol; 84mg Sodium.
Points: 2

Scallop Saute Provencals

Wash and dry scallops and cut in pieces, if large, then roll in flour. Heat oil, add scallops and cook quickly-tossing at all times for 5 min. While cooking add garlic, mix well, then add salt and pepper to taste. Just before taking pan from stove add parsley. Serve with lemon wedges.

Servings: 4
Start to finish: 30 minutes

1 1/2 pounds scallop, bay & sea
1/2 cup flour
6 tablespoons olive oil
3 cloves garlic fine chopped
salt and pepper, to taste
1/2 cup parsley, chopped

Nutritional Values:
Per Serving (excluding unknown items): 242 Calories; 20g Fat (75.3% calories from fat); 2g Protein; 13g Carbohydrate; 1g Dietary Fiber; 0mg Cholesterol; 5mg Sodium.
Points: 6

Substitute Values:
Per Serving (using substitute enova cooking oil): 65 Calories; trace Fat (6.3% calories from fat); 2g Protein; 13g Carbohydrate; 1g Dietary Fiber; 0mg Cholesterol; 5mg Sodium.
Points: 1

Roy's Fish Sauce

Heat in sauce pan and cool. Keep in refrigerator. Perfect to use for barbecuing salmon chunks.

Servings: 8
Start to finish: 10 minutes

1/2 lb. Butter
1 clove garlic Chopped
1/4 teaspoon garlic powder
4 tablespoons soy sauce
1 tablespoons mustard
1/4 cup ketchup
1/4 Worcestershire sauce

Nutritional Values:
Per Serving (excluding unknown items): 224 Calories; 23g Fat (90.3% calories from fat); 1g Protein; 4g Carbohydrate; trace Dietary Fiber; 62mg Cholesterol; 935mg Sodium.
Points: 6

Substitute Values:
Per Serving (using substitute): 119 Calories; 11g Fat (81.8% calories from fat); 1g Protein; 5g Carbohydrate; trace Dietary Fiber; 0mg Cholesterol; 973mg Sodium.
Points: 3

Clam Sauce
Venetian Style

Saute garlic in oil and butter 5 mins. Add rest of ingredients. Simmer 20 min. stirring occasionally. To make red clam sauce add 2 tomato puree when adding clams etc.

Serving Ideas: Delicious with green salad, French bread and sherbet. Tip: Use lemon over spaghetti rather than cheese.

Servings: 4
Start to finish: 30 minutes
Yield: 6 cups

13 ounces clams, minced
(2 cans at 6.5 oz.)
8 ounces clam juice, jar
3 cloves garlic, minced
1/2 cup cooking oil
1 tablespoon butter
pepper, freshly ground
1/2 cup parsley, chopped fine
1 teaspoon basil
1/2 teaspoon oregano
1/2 tablespoon red pepper, crushed
(optional)

Nutritional Values:
Per Serving (excluding unknown items): 342 Calories; 31g Fat (81.2% calories from fat); 12g Protein; 4g Carbohydrate; 1g Dietary Fiber; 39mg Cholesterol; 86mg Sodium.
Points: 9

Substitute Values:
Per Serving (using substitute Enova Cooking Oil and imitation margarine): 91 Calories; 3g Fat (26.8% calories from fat); 12g Protein; 4g Carbohydrate; 1g Dietary Fiber; 31mg Cholesterol; 91mg Sodium.
Points: 2

Crab Cakes

Pick crab meat out of shelled meat or imitation crab shelled. Mix together bread, mayonnaise, mustard and seasonings.. Add crab meat and mix gently but thoroughly. If mixture is too dry add ¼ cup milk. Shape into cakes and bread with dry bread crumbs. Deep fry for 3-5 minutes or until browned. Can also be pan fried until brown, a few minutes on each side.

Servings: 4
Start to finish: 30 minutes

1 pound crab meat
2 cups bread cubes, small pieces
2 tablespoons mayonnaise
3 tablespoons horseradish
3 tablespoons mustard, prepared
1/2 teaspoon salt
1/4 teaspoon pepper
1 teaspoon Worcestershire sauce
dash tabasco sauce
1 tablespoon parsley, chopped
1 whole egg

Nutritional Values:
Per Serving (excluding unknown items): 255 Calories; 10g Fat (35.1% calories from fat); 28g Protein; 13g Carbohydrate; 1g Dietary Fiber; 156mg Cholesterol; 997mg Sodium.
Points: 6

Substitute Values:
Per Serving (using substitute): 211 Calories; 4g Fat (17.4% calories from fat); 27g Protein; 15g Carbohydrate; 1g Dietary Fiber; 154mg Cholesterol; 1053mg Sodium.
Points: 4

Crab Egg Foo Young

Combine eggs, sprouts, onions, crab meat, pepper, garlic salt, mixing lightly. Oil large frying pan and fry as if you were making small pancakes. Serve hot with sauce. Combine cornstarch, sugar, soy sauce, vinegar and chicken stock and cook over low heat until thickened.

Servings: 4
Start to finish: 30-40 minutes

8 whole eggs, beaten well
15 ounces bean sprouts
2/3 cup green onion, thinly sliced
2 cups crab meat, cooked
1/4 teaspoon pepper
1/4 teaspoon garlic powder
2 tablespoons cooking oil
salt, to taste

Sauce:
2 teaspoons cornstarch
2 teaspoons sugar
4 teaspoons soy sauce
2 teaspoons vinegar
1 cup chicken stock

Nutritional Values:
Per Serving (excluding unknown items): 335 Calories; 18g Fat (48.2% calories from fat); 31g Protein; 13g Carbohydrate; 2g Dietary Fiber; 484mg Cholesterol; 1254mg Sodium.
Points: 8

Substitute Values:
Per Serving (using substitute enova cooking oil, 99% egg substitute sugar substitute, and fat free chicken stock): 221 Calories; 1g Fat (5.4% calories from fat); 37g Protein; 14g Carbohydrate; 2g Dietary Fiber; 60mg Cholesterol; 1032mg Sodium.
Points: 4

Casseroles

Casseroles

Crab Spinach Casserole

Cook spinach slightly- drain well. Arrange in bottom of greased casserole. Sprinkle with half the cheese. Cover with crab meat, grated onion, lemon juice and cover with remaining cheese.
Sauce: Melt butter, blend flour, add tomato soup. Cook until slightly thickened. Stir in sour cream. Pour over mixture in casserole. Dot with butter. Bake in moderate oven 30 min.

Servings: 6
Start to finish: 60 minutes

24 ounces spinach, frozen, chopped and dried
1/2 pound sharp cheddar cheese, grated
2 cups crab meat
1 tablespoon onion, grated
1 tablespoon lemon juice
2 tablespoons butter
2 tablespoons flour
10 3/4 ounces tomato soup
1 cup sour cream

Nutritional Values:
Per Serving (excluding unknown items): 369 Calories; 26g Fat (61.4% calories from fat); 24g Protein; 12g Carbohydrate; 4g Dietary Fiber; 107mg Cholesterol; 673mg Sodium.
Points: 9

Substitute Values:
Per Serving (using substitute fat-free cheddar cheese, margarine imitation, tomato soup, reduced fat, condensed): 218 Calories; 3g Fat (13.8% calories from fat); 28g Protein; 20g Carbohydrate; 4g Dietary Fiber; 51mg Cholesterol; 776mg Sodium.
Points: 4

Chicken Rice Casserole

Blend together rice, soup and milk. Pour mixture into casserole dish and place chicken pieces or parts on top of above ingredients. Sprinkle a package of onion soup mix on top. Cover with foil and bake for 2 ½ hours.

Servings: 6
Start to finish: 2:40 minutes

2 pounds chicken breast
1 1/3 cups rice, instant
10 3/4 ounces cream of celery soup
10 3/4 ounces cream of mushroom soup
1/2 cup milk
1 package onion soup mix

Nutritional Values:
Per Serving (excluding unknown items): 346 Calories; 15g Fat (39.9% calories from fat); 28g Protein; 22g Carbohydrate; 1g Dietary Fiber; 84mg Cholesterol; 500mg Sodium.
Points: 8

Substitute Values:
Per Serving (using substitute rice, short-grain, Cream of Celery 98% fat free, cream of mushroom soup fat free): 375 Calories; 11g Fat (28.4% calories from fat); 29g Protein; 36g Carbohydrate; 1g Dietary Fiber; 78mg Cholesterol; 90mg Sodium.
Points: 8

Poulet D' Artichokes

Cook artichokes according to package directions adding a little olive oil and 2 garlic cloves. Drain cooked artichokes and arrange in a greased baking dish. Spread chicken on top of the artichokes. Combine and mix well the soup, mayonnaise, lemon juice and curry powder. Pour over the chicken. Sprinkle with grated cheese. Toss bread cubes in melted butter to coat. Scatter on top of cheese. Bake at 350° for 25 min. Can be made ahead and cooked later.

Servings: 8
Start to finish: 35 minutes

18 ounces frozen artichoke heart
2 2/3 cups chicken, cubed
21 1/2 ounces cream of chicken soup (2 cans)
1 cup mayonnaise
1 teaspoon lemon juice
1/2 teaspoon curry powder
1 1/4 cups sharp cheddar cheese, shredded
1 1/4 cups bread cubes, small cubes
2 cloves garlic, chopped

Nutritional Values:
Per Serving (excluding unknown items): 478 Calories; 41g Fat (75.5% calories from fat); 18g Protein; 12g Carbohydrate; 4g Dietary Fiber; 83mg Cholesterol; 696mg Sodium.
Points: 12

Substitute Values:
Per Serving (using substitute cream of chicken soup 98% fat-free, fat-free mayonnaise, fat-free cheddar cheese): 223 Calories; 10g Fat (39.2% calories from fat); 18g Protein; 16g Carbohydrate; 4g Dietary Fiber; 55mg Cholesterol; 629mg Sodium.
Points: 4

Green Stuffed Olive Enchiladas

Stuff and roll tortillas with sour cream, olives and onion. Pour enchilada sauce (small amount) in pan and then over the top and bake 25min. at 350°. Serve with avocado mashed on top.

Servings: 3
Start to finish: 40 minutes

6 corn tortilla
1 cup sour cream
1 whole onion, large chopped fine
4 ounces green olives, jar
1 cup cheddar cheese, grated
1 ounce enchilada sauce, canned

Nutritional Values:
Per Serving (excluding unknown items): 468 Calories; 36g Fat (78.2% calories from fat); 13g Protein; 10g Carbohydrate; 4g Dietary Fiber; 77mg Cholesterol; 617mg Sodium.
Points: 12

Substitute Values:
Per Serving (using substitute fat-free cheddar cheese, fat-free sour cream): 256 Calories; 7g Fat (31.6% calories from fat); 19g Protein; 16g Carbohydrate; 4g Dietary Fiber; 18mg Cholesterol; 669mg Sodium.
Points: 5

Hamburger Cheese Bake

In skillet brown beef and onion. Stir in tomato sauce, sugar, salt, garlic salt and pepper. Remove from heat. Cook noodles and drain. Combine cottage cheese, cream cheese, sour cream, green onions, and green pepper. Spread half noodles on 9x13" baking dish. Top with cheese mixture. Add remaining noodles and meat sauce. Sprinkle with Parmesan cheese. Bake in 350° oven for 30 min.

Servings: 4
Start to finish: 60 minutes

1 pound ground round
1 medium onion, chopped
16 ounces tomato sauce
1 teaspoon sugar
3/4 teaspoon salt
1/4 teaspoon garlic salt
1/4 teaspoon pepper
12 ounces egg noodles
8 ounces cottage cheese, creamed
8 ounces cream cheese
1/4 cup sour cream
1/3 cup green pepper, chopped
1/4 cup Parmesan cheese

Nutritional Values:
Per Serving (excluding unknown items): 635 Calories; 33g Fat (47.2% calories from fat); 33g Protein; 51g Carbohydrate; 3g Dietary Fiber; 160mg Cholesterol; 1204mg Sodium.
Points: 15

Substitute Values:
Per Serving (using substitute ground beef, 95% lean, sugar substitute, fat-free cottage cheese, fat-free cream cheese, fat-free sour cream, and fat-free Parmesan cheese): 518 Calories; 5g Fat (11.3% calories from fat); 29g Protein; 54g Carbohydrate; 3g Dietary Fiber; 84mg Cholesterol; 1195mg Sodium.
Points: 10

Macaroni Chili

Mix all ingredients together. Put in 13x9" casserole dish. Bake at 325° ½ hour. Stir and sprinkle with Parmesan cheese. Bake ½ hour longer at 325°

Servings: 8
Preparation Time: 20 minutes
Start to finish: 1 hour 20 minutes

2 whole eggs
2 cups elbow macaroni, cooked
2 1/2 cups milk
1/2 pound cheddar cheese
1 tablespoon green pepper
1 tablespoon onion, grated
1 clove garlic, chopped
1 1/2 tablespoons chili powder
1 cup olives, sliced

Nutritional Values:
Per Serving (excluding unknown items): 258 Calories; 15g Fat (53.6% calories from fat); 13g Protein; 17g Carbohydrate; 1g Dietary Fiber; 93mg Cholesterol; 394mg Sodium.
Points: 6

Substitute Values:
Per Serving (using substitute fat free milk and cheese): 164 Calories; 4g Fat (19.8% calories from fat); 15g Protein; 18g Carbohydrate; 1g Dietary Fiber; 59mg Cholesterol; 422mg Sodium.
Points: 3

Stuffed Mushrooms Thomas

Saute ground chuck and green onions set aside. Cook spinach as directed on package and mix with cheeses, sour cream, green onion tops, salt, and herb seasoning. Butter a large casserole. Place the 12 large mushrooms, cup side up, in casserole. Spread meat mixture over the mushrooms, then spoon spinach mixture over all. Top with ½ cup cheddar and ½ cup jack cheese. Bake at 350° for 25 min.

Servings: 6
Start to finish: 40 minutes

1 1/2 pounds ground chuck
1/4 cup green onions, sliced
16 ounces frozen spinach, chopped
1 cup sour cream
1/2 cup cheddar cheese, shredded
1/2 cup monterey jack cheese, shredded
1/2 cup green onion , tops
1 1/2 teaspoons salt
1 teaspoon italian seasoning, herb
12 large mushrooms caps

Nutritional Values:
Per Serving (excluding unknown items): 475 Calories; 38g Fat (71.7% calories from fat); 28g Protein; 5g Carbohydrate; 2g Dietary Fiber; 120mg Cholesterol; 797mg Sodium.
Points: 12

Substitute Values:
Per Serving (using substitute ground beef 95% lean, fat-free sour cream, fat-free cheddar cheese and Monterey jack cheese low fat): 345 Calories; 3g Fat (18.8% calories from fat); 19g Protein; 8g Carbohydrate; 2g Dietary Fiber; 37mg Cholesterol; 719mg Sodium.
Points: 7

Ham Loaf

Mix ham, pork, milk , eggs, and bread crumbs together and put in loaf pan or casserole. Mix brown sugar, water, vinegar and mustard to create glaze. Bake 1 ½ hours at 350° glazing with sauce and basting frequently. It's best to bake 2 loaves then one can be frozen for later if not used.

Servings: 12
Preparation Time: 20 minutes
Start to finish: 1 hour 50 minutes

2 pounds smoked Ham
1 1/2 pounds pork
1 cup milk
2 whole eggs, beaten
1 cup bread crumbs, fine dry
3/4 cup brown sugar
1/4 cup water
1/4 cup vinegar
2 teaspoons dry mustard

Nutritional Values:
Per Serving (excluding unknown items): 96 Calories; 2g Fat (19.1% calories from fat); 3g Protein; 17g Carbohydrate; trace Dietary Fiber; 38mg Cholesterol; 103mg Sodium.
Points: 2

Substitute Values:
Per Serving (using substitute skim milk): 91 Calories; 1g Fat (14.0% calories from fat); 3g Protein; 17g Carbohydrate; trace Dietary Fiber; 36mg Cholesterol; 104mg Sodium.
Points: 2

Chili Relleno Casserole

Remove chili seeds and flatten chilies to cover bottom of baking dish, 13"x 9". Cover with cheddar and more chilies, then jack cheese. Separate eggs, set egg whites aside, and add 3 tablespoons flour to egg yolks. Add half and half salt and pepper to taste. Beat until mixed. Beat egg whites stiff. Mix with yolks. Pour over cheese mixture. Bake 350° for 45min. Pour chili salsa over top and bake 30 min longer.

Servings: 8
Preparation Time: 30 minutes
Start to finish: 1 hour

16 ounces chili pepper, canned
1 pound cheddar cheese
1 pound Monterey jack cheese
4 whole eggs
1 pint half and half
7 1/2 ounces green chili salsa, canned
1 tablespoon flour

Nutritional Values:
Per Serving (excluding unknown items): 572 Calories; 45g Fat (71.4% calories from fat); 34g Protein; 8g Carbohydrate; 1g Dietary Fiber; 238mg Cholesterol; 1381mg Sodium.
Points: 15

Substitute Values:
Per Serving (using substitute fat-free cheddar cheese, and Monterey jack cheese low fat): 174 Calories; 3g Fat (14.6% calories from fat); 22g Protein; 12g Carbohydrate; 1g Dietary Fiber; 116mg Cholesterol; 1165mg Sodium.
Points: 4

Tamale Pie

Saute onions and garlic. Mix in with remaining ingredients. Put grated cheese on top and place in baking dish at 350° for 1 to 1 ½ hours. You can add chili powder or cumin for more flavor.

Servings: 4
Start to finish: 2:00 hours

16 ounces tamales, chopped, canned
8 fluid ounces tomato sauce, canned
5 3/8 ounces corn, creamed
1/2 cup milk
1/2 cup cheddar cheese
1/2 cup olives, chopped
salt and pepper, to taste
1/2 cup cornmeal
1 whole eggs, beaten
1 clove garlic, 1/2" cubes
1/4 cup onion, chopped

Nutritional Values:
Per Serving (excluding unknown items): 372 Calories; 17g Fat (41.7% calories from fat); 14g Protein; 41g Carbohydrate; 7g Dietary Fiber; 82mg Cholesterol; 1402mg Sodium.
Points: 8

Substitute Values:
Per Serving (using substitute): 327 Calories; 12g Fat (32.0% calories from fat); 15g Protein; 41g Carbohydrate; 7g Dietary Fiber; 66mg Cholesterol; 1416mg Sodium.
Points: 7

Baked Ham Omelet

Take white bread – cut off crusts, butter well, and cut in cubes. Put in 9"x13" pan. ½ lb. Grated cheddar cheese over bread. ½ lb. Cubed ham over cheese. Beat together 6 eggs, 3 cups milk and ¼ teaspoon salt. Pour over casserole. Refrigerate overnight. Bake at 325° 55 min. Let stand 5 to 10 min. before cutting. This can be reheated.

Servings: 10
Preparation Time: Several hours or overnight
Start to finish: 1 hour

12 slices white bread
5/8 pound cheddar cheese
7 1/2 whole eggs
3 3/4 cups milk
1/3 teaspoon salt
1 1/4 pounds ham, cubed
2 tablespoons butter, for bread

Nutritional Values:
Per Serving (excluding unknown items): 430 Calories; 26g Fat (54.1% calories from fat); 27g Protein; 22g Carbohydrate; 1g Dietary Fiber; 240mg Cholesterol; 1272mg Sodium.
Points: 11

Substitute Values:
Per Serving (using substitute fat-free cheddar cheese, egg substitute, and skim milk): 304 Calories; 8g Fat (25.4% calories from fat); 32g Protein; 24g Carbohydrate; 1g Dietary Fiber; 39mg Cholesterol; 1381mg Sodium.
Points: 7

Mock Ravioli Casserole

#1 Sauce Mix:

2 med. Onion, 1 clove crushed garlic, 3 T oil, 2 lb. Ground beef, 10oz can mushrooms, 1/8oz. Can tomato sauce, 1 can tomato paste, 1 ½ C water, 1 ½ tsp Italian herbs, salt and pepper to taste. Saute onions and garlic, add meat, cook until brown. Add reaming ingredients, cover and simmer slowly for two hours.

#2 Spinach Mix:

½ C salad oil, 2 pkg. Frozen chopped spinach (defrosted), ½ C minced parsley, 1 C soft bread crumbs, ½ C grated cheese Parmesan cheese, 1 clove garlic chopped, 1 tsp sage, 1 tsp salt, 4 well beaten eggs. Mix well.

#3

Cook 1 lb. Butterfly or seashell macaroni as directed till tender, drain well. In large greased baking dish, layer cooked macaroni, top with layer of spinach mix, add meat mix and top with cheese.

Bake at 350° for 30-40 min.

Servings: 10
Start to finish: 60 minutes

2 medium onion
1 clove garlic, crushed
3 tablespoons oil
2 pounds ground beef
10 ounces mushroom, canned
8 ounces tomato sauce, canned
6 ounces tomato paste
1 1/2 cups water
1 1/2 teaspoons Italian seasoning
salt and pepper, to taste
1/2 cup oil
32 ounces spinach, frozen chopped
1/2 cup parsley, minced
1 cup soft bread crumbs
1/2 cup Parmesan cheese, grated
1 clove garlic, chopped
1 teaspoon sage
1 teaspoon salt
4 whole egg, beaten
1 pound macaroni, or seashell macaroni cooked

Nutritional Values:
Per Serving (excluding unknown items): 701 Calories; 44g Fat (55.8% calories from fat); 30g Protein; 48g Carbohydrate; 6g Dietary Fiber; 165mg Cholesterol; 753mg Sodium.
Points: 17

Substitute Values:
Per Serving (using substitute enova cooking oil , egg substitute and fat free cheese): 504 Calories; 4g Fat (9.9% calories from fat); 25g Protein; 51g Carbohydrate; 6g Dietary Fiber; 30mg Cholesterol; 726mg Sodium.
Points: 10

Noodle Bake

Brown ground beef, add tomato sauce, salt, pepper and basil to taste. Combine cottage cheese, cream cheese, sour cream, chopped scallion and green pepper. Cook noodles, drain and toss with butter. Place ½ noodles in bottom of casserole, cover with cheese mixture, more noodles, then meat sauce over all. Bake at 375° for 20 min.

Servings: 6
Preparation Time: 20 minutes
Start to finish: 40 minutes

1 pound ground beef
16 ounces tomato sauce
salt and pepper, to taste
basil , to taste
1 cup cottage cheese, cheese
8 ounces cream cheese
1/2 cup sour cream
2 whole scallions, chopped
1 cup green pepper, chopped
1/2 pound noodles, drained
2 tablespoons butter

Nutritional Values:
Per Serving (excluding unknown items): 650 Calories; 44g Fat (60.0% calories from fat); 28g Protein; 37g Carbohydrate; 3g Dietary Fiber; 164mg Cholesterol; 832mg Sodium.
Points: 16

Substitute Values:
Per Serving (using substitute ground beef 95% lean, fat-free cottage cheese, fat-free cream cheese, fat-free sour cream, and margarine imitation): 455 Calories; 6g Fat (16.7% calories from fat); 26g Protein; 40g Carbohydrate; 3g Dietary Fiber; 63mg Cholesterol; 855mg Sodium.
Points: 9

Asparagus n' Ham Crepes

Steam asparagus 10-15 min. until crisp and tender. Place 1 ham slice, 1 cheese slice and 3-4 spears of asparagus on each crepe and roll. Place crepe in large shallow baking dish. Spoon mushroom wine sauce over top of crepes. Bake in preheated 350° oven 20 to 30 min.

Wine Sauce: Saute mushrooms in butter until tender. Stir in flour. Add chicken broth, wine, chives and horseradish; cook over medium heat, stirring constantly until thickened. Stir in cream.

Servings: 6
Start to finish: 1:30 minutes

12 ounces ham slice, 1 oz per slice
2 pounds asparagus,
cleaned and trimmed
12 slices Swiss cheese slices
12 Crepes', (Basic Crepe Recipe)

Wine Sauce:
3 cups mushrooms, sliced
3 tablespoons butter
3 tablespoons flour
3/4 cup chicken broth
1/4 cup Madeira wine or Vermouth
1 tablespoon chives, chopped
1 teaspoon horseradish
1/4 cup cream

Nutritional Values:
Per Serving (excluding unknown items): 482 Calories; 35g Fat (64.6% calories from fat); 30g Protein; 13g Carbohydrate; 2g Dietary Fiber; 115mg Cholesterol; 1095mg Sodium.
Points: 12

Substitute Values:
Per Serving (using substitute): 569 Calories; 18g Fat (28.4% calories from fat); 81g Protein; 20g Carbohydrate; 2g Dietary Fiber; 106mg Cholesterol; 1560mg Sodium.
Points: 12

Breads and Sandwiches

BREADS AND SANDWICHES

Banana Honey Bran Bread

Sift flour, baking powder, soda and salt into large bowl. Stir in cereal. Set aside. Beat eggs, honey, oil, milk and banana. Add all at once to flour mixture, till dampened. Spoon into greased loaf pan. Bake at 350° 40 -45min. Cool 10 min. remove from pan. I like a little raisins added.

Servings: 8
Start to finish: 1 hour

1 1/2 cup flour
2 teaspoon baking powder
1/2 teaspoon baking soda
1/2 teaspoon salt
1 cup whole bran cereal
1 1/2 cups mashed ripe bananas
1 egg
1/2 cup honey
1/4 cup cooking oil
1/4 cup milk

Nutritional Values:
Per Serving (excluding unknown items): 263 Calories; 8g Fat (26.8% calories from fat); 4g Protein; 46g Carbohydrate; 2g Dietary Fiber; 28mg Cholesterol; 348mg Sodium.
Points: 6

Substitute Values:
Per Serving (using substitute enova cooking oil and skim milk): 202 Calories; 1g Fat (5.1% calories from fat); 4g Protein; 46g Carbohydrate; 2g Dietary Fiber; 27mg Cholesterol; 348mg Sodium.
Points: 4

Sour Dough Garlic Cheese Bread

Cut open, into halves, sour dough loaf. First spread butter or margarine generously on open halves of bread. Then spread on top of butter the garlic spread generously mixing both. Pour the Parmesan cheese on top of butter mixture and pat into loaf halves and shake off excess cheese. Sprinkle paprika lightly on top of open halves and bake at 380° for 14-17 min. until top is golden brown. Take out and cut diagonally.

Servings: 10
Start to finish: 30 minutes

1 sour dough loaf
4 ounces Lawry's® garlic spread
1/4 cup butter, or margarine softened
3/4 cup Parmesan cheese
paprika, for garnish

Nutritional Values:
Per Serving (excluding unknown items): 149 Calories; 7g Fat (85.9% calories from fat); 3g Protein; trace Carbohydrate; 1g Dietary Fiber; 17mg Cholesterol; 159mg Sodium.
Points: 3

Substitute Values:
Per Serving (using substitute): 122 Calories; 3g Fat (56.2% calories from fat); 3g Protein; 3g Carbohydrate; 1g Dietary Fiber; 7mg Cholesterol; 120mg Sodium.
Points: 2

Cranberry Bread

Sift together dry ingredients. Add cranberries, nuts, butter, and orange juice. Bake at 350° for 1 hour.

Servings: 10
Start to finish: 60 minutes

2 cups sifted flour
1/2 teaspoon baking powder
1/2 teaspoon baking soda
1 cup sugar

1 cup cranberries, ground
3/4 cup nuts, chopped
3 tablespoons butter, melted
1/3 cup orange juice, add water to make 3/4 cup

Nutritional Values:
Per Serving (excluding unknown items): 266 Calories; 10g Fat (32.1% calories from fat); 4g Protein; 42g Carbohydrate; 2g Dietary Fiber; 9mg Cholesterol; 124mg Sodium.
Points: 10

Substitute Values:
Per Serving (using substitute no nuts, margarine imitation and sugar substitute): 146 Calories; 2g Fat (12.4% calories from fat); 2g Protein; 28g Carbohydrate; 1g Dietary Fiber; 0mg Cholesterol; 168mg Sodium.
Points: 1

Peanut Butter Yogurt Bread

Combine the peanut butter, sugar and egg in a large bowl and mix well. Stir in the butter, yogurt and orange rind and mix again. Sift the flour, baking soda, baking powder, and salt into the peanut butter mixture and stir to combine ingredients. Turn into loaf pan 9x5x3, and bake at 350° for 1 hour or until done. Cool about 5 min. and place on rack.

Servings: 10
Start to finish: 1:30 minutes

1/2 cup peanut butter
1/3 cup sugar
1 whole egg
1 tablespoon butter
1 cup yogurt, plain
1 teaspoon orange rind, grated
2 cups all-purpose flour
1 teaspoon baking soda
1 teaspoon baking powder
1/2 teaspoon salt
1/2 cup peanuts, chopped

Nutritional Values:
Per Serving (excluding unknown items): 268 Calories; 13g Fat (42.0% calories from fat); 9g Protein; 31g Carbohydrate; 2g Dietary Fiber; 27mg Cholesterol; 373mg Sodium.
Points: 6

Substitute Values:
Per Serving (using substitute): 247 Calories; 12g Fat (42.0% calories from fat); 10g Protein; 27g Carbohydrate; 2g Dietary Fiber; 3mg Cholesterol; 398mg Sodium.
Points: 6

Zucchini Bread

Beat eggs, add oil, sugar, zucchini and vanilla. Mix lightly , but well. Add flour, salt, baking powder, baking soda and cinnamon. Mix until blended. Bake at 325° for 1 hour.

Makes 2 loaves
Servings: 16
Start to finish: 1:20 minutes

3 whole eggs
2 1/2 cups sugar
2 cups zucchini, grated and peeled
3 cups flour
1/4 teaspoon baking powder
3 teaspoons cinnamon
1 cup oil
3 teaspoons vanilla
1 teaspoon salt
1 teaspoon baking soda
1/2 cup nuts

Nutritional Values:
Per Serving (excluding unknown items): 399 Calories; 18g Fat (41.2% calories from fat); 5g Protein; 55g Carbohydrate; 2g Dietary Fiber; 42mg Cholesterol; 250mg Sodium.
Points: 9

Substitute Values:
Per Serving (using substitute no nuts, Enova cooking oil, sugar substitute, and egg substitute): 172 Calories; trace Fat (1.9% calories from fat); 5g Protein; 35g Carbohydrate; 1g Dietary Fiber; 0mg Cholesterol; 333mg Sodium.
Points: 3

Pumpkin Bread

Combine sugar, pumpkin, oil and eggs; beat until well blended. Sift together flour, soda, salt and spices. Add to first mixture and mix well. Stir in raisins, nuts and water. Spoon into well oiled 9x5x3 loaf pan. Bake at 350° for 65-75 min. or until done when tested with a toothpick. Turn out onto rack to cool.

Servings: 16
Yield: 2 loaves
Start to finish: 2 hours 10 minutes

1 cup brown sugar
1/2 cup sugar
1 cup pumpkin, cooked canned
1/2 cup oil
2 whole eggs, unbeaten
2 cups sifted all purpose flour
1 teaspoon salt
1/2 teaspoon nutmeg
1 teaspoon cinnamon
1 teaspoon baking soda
1/4 teaspoon ginger
1 cup raisins
1 teaspoon ground cloves
1 cup nuts, chopped
1/4 cup water

Nutritional Values:
Per Serving (excluding unknown items): 265 Calories; 13g Fat (41.6% calories from fat); 4g Protein; 36g Carbohydrate; 2g Dietary Fiber; 27mg Cholesterol; 227mg Sodium.
Points: 6

Substitute Values:
Per Serving (using substitute no nuts, Enova cooking oil, sugar substitutes, and egg substitute): 101 Calories; trace Fat (2.7% calories from fat); 3g Protein; 22g Carbohydrate; 1g Dietary Fiber; 0mg Cholesterol; 247mg Sodium.
Points: 2

Zucchini Torte

Beat eggs. Add oil. Add seasonings and Bis quick. Stir. Blend in zucchini, cheese and onion. Pour into 9x12 pan. Bake at 350° for 30-35 min. Can be frozen and reheated.

Servings: 8
Preparation Time: 20 minutes
Start to finish: 1 hour

5 whole eggs
1/4 cup oil
2 teaspoons garlic powder
1/4 teaspoon pepper
dash Tabasco sauce
1 1/2 cups cheddar cheese, grated
1 1/2 cups Bis quick® baking mix
1 whole onion, chopped
1 teaspoon salt
1/4 teaspoon oregano
4 cups zucchini, thinly sliced

Nutritional Values:
Per Serving (excluding unknown items): 299 Calories; 20g Fat (60.0% calories from fat); 12g Protein; 18g Carbohydrate; 2g Dietary Fiber; 155mg Cholesterol; 707mg Sodium.
Points: 7

Substitute Values:
Per Serving (using substitute Enova cooking oil, and egg substitute): 169 Calories; 3g Fat (17.2% calories from fat); 15g Protein; 20g Carbohydrate; 2g Dietary Fiber; 4mg Cholesterol; 790mg Sodium.
Points: 3

Challah
(Egg Bread)

Combine yeast, water, sugar and let stand for 5 min. Add to yeast mixture eggs, oil, salt and flour and knead for 5 mins. Place in bowl and let rise 2 hours. Punch down and let rise for 1 hour. Place on bread board. Divide into 3 balls. Elongate into strips. Braid. Place on cookie sheet (greased). Mix 1 egg yolk with 1 T water. Brush on braided loaf. Sprinkle with sesame seed. Let rise 1 hour. Bake in preheated oven 350° for 35 min.

Servings: 8
Start to finish: 4:35 minutes

1 package yeast
(either fresh or powder)
1 1/2 cups warm water
2 tablespoons sugar

Add:
2 whole eggs
2 tablespoons oil
2 teaspoons salt
4 1/2 cups all-purpose flour

Nutritional Values:
Per Serving (excluding unknown items): 319 Calories; 5g Fat (15.4% calories from fat); 9g Protein; 57g Carbohydrate; 2g Dietary Fiber; 53mg Cholesterol; 554mg Sodium.
Points: 6

Substitute Values:
Per Serving (using substitute Enova cooking oil, sugar substitutes, and egg substitute): 278 Calories; 1g Fat (2.8% calories from fat); 10g Protein; 56g Carbohydrate; 2g Dietary Fiber; 0mg Cholesterol; 585mg Sodium.
Points: 5

Mexican Spoon Bread

Mix batter and pour half in 9"x9" baking dish. Cover with chilies and half the grated cheese. Add balance of batter and top with remainder of cheese. Bake at 350° for 45min. until golden brown on top. Cut in squares and serve hot.

Servings: 8
Start to finish: 60 minutes

14 1/2 ounces creamed corn, canned
3/4 cup milk
1/3 cup oil
pinch salt
2 whole eggs, beaten
1 cup yellow cornmeal
1/2 teaspoon baking soda
4 ounces chilies, green chopped
1 1/2 cups cheddar cheese, grated

Nutritional Values:
Per Serving (excluding unknown items): 299 Calories; 19g Fat (55.1% calories from fat); 10g Protein; 24g Carbohydrate; 2g Dietary Fiber; 78mg Cholesterol; 386mg Sodium.
Points: 7

Substitute Values:
Per Serving (using substitute Enova cooking oil, milk substitutes, and egg substitute, fat free cheddar cheese): 152 Calories; 1g Fat (3.8% calories from fat); 12g Protein; 25g Carbohydrate; 2g Dietary Fiber; 4mg Cholesterol; 432mg Sodium.
Points: 3

Western Cheese Buns

Combine ingredients and spread mixture on open face hamburger buns and melt cheese under broiler.

Servings: 6
Start to finish: 30 minutes

1/2 pound cheddar cheese, shredded
2 tablespoons green pepper, chopped
2 tablespoons onion, chopped
2 whole eggs, hard boiled and chopped
1/4 cup green olives, stuffed and chopped
1 teaspoon prepared mustard
3 tablespoons chili sauce
salt and pepper, to taste
3 hamburger buns or whole wheat buns

Nutritional Values:
Per Serving (excluding unknown items): 249 Calories; 16g Fat (57.8% calories from fat); 14g Protein; 13g Carbohydrate; 1g Dietary Fiber; 110mg Cholesterol; 440mg Sodium.
Points: 6

Substitute Values:
Per Serving (using substitute fat free cheddar cheese and egg substitute and whole wheat buns): 151 Calories; 2g Fat (10.0% calories from fat); 18g Protein; 15g Carbohydrate; 2g Dietary Fiber; 7mg Cholesterol; 473mg Sodium.
Points: 3

Cottage Cheese Dill Bread

Sprinkle yeast in warm water; stir until blended ; stir in 2 teaspoons sugar, set aside. Combine cottage cheese, onion, dill weed, baking powder, salt, 2 tablespoons sugar and eggs. Mix thoroughly. Add yeast mixture and mix well. Add flour to make a stiff dough. Knead on lightly flour surface until smooth and elastic. Place dough in greased bowl; turn to bring greased side up. Cover; let rise in warm place until doubled in size (1 ½ hours). Punch down. Turn out onto lightly floured surface; knead a few times. Divide into two equal portions. Shape each portion into loaves and place in well greased loaf pans 8"x5"x3". Bake at 350° for 30 min. Remove from pans to rack. If desired, brush tops with melted butter or margarine.

Servings: 8
Start to finish: 2:30 minutes

2 packages dry yeast, active
1/2 cup water, warm
2 tablespoons sugar
2 cups cottage cheese, creamed
2 tablespoons onion, minced
2 tablespoons dill weed
1 teaspoon baking powder
2 teaspoons salt
2 tablespoons sugar
2 whole eggs
4 1/2 cups all purpose flour

Nutritional Values:
Per Serving (excluding unknown items): 105 Calories; 4g Fat (31.6% calories from fat); 9g Protein; 9g Carbohydrate; 1g Dietary Fiber; 61mg Cholesterol; 827mg Sodium.
Points: 2

Substitute Values:
Per Serving (using substitute low fat creamed cheese, sugar substitutes, and egg substitute): 84 Calories; 1g Fat (13.3% calories from fat); 11g Protein; 7g Carbohydrate; 1g Dietary Fiber; 5mg Cholesterol; 881mg Sodium.
Points: 2

Baked Alaskan Crab Sandwich

Spread butter on muffins halves and toast in oven. Combine crab, celery, 5 tablespoons mayonnaise, mustard, and salt. Place mixture on muffin halves. Fold in 1 tablespoons mayonnaise into 2 egg whites. Spread over crab mixture, sealing edges. Bake at 450° till topping is slightly browned.

Servings: 8
Start to finish: 30 minutes

4 whole English muffins
2 tablespoons margarine
6 ounces crab meat, (snow crab meat thawed and drained)
3/4 cup celery, diced
6 tablespoons mayonnaise
2 teaspoons prepared mustard
1/2 teaspoon salt
2 egg whites beaten stiff

Nutritional Values:
Per Serving (excluding unknown items): 206 Calories; 14g Fat (58.7% calories from fat); 8g Protein; 14g Carbohydrate; 1g Dietary Fiber; 73mg Cholesterol; 463mg Sodium.
Points: 5

Substitute Values:
Per Serving (using substitute whole wheat muffins, fat free mayonnaise and margarine substitute): 128 Calories; 4g Fat (24.9% calories from fat); 8g Protein; 16g Carbohydrate; 2g Dietary Fiber; 70mg Cholesterol; 626mg Sodium.
Points: 3

Crab Salad Sandwiches

Combine crab meat, celery, onion, green pepper and onion. Put crab mixture between slices of unbuttered bread and place in 9"x13" baking dish. Combine in sauce pan butter, flour, onion, milk cheddar cheese and salt and pepper until melted. Pour cheese sauce over sandwiches in baking dish, refrigerate at least 2 hours or overnight. Bake at 350° for ½ to 1 hour.

Servings: 6
Preparation Time: 30 minutes
Start to finish: 3 hours

Notes: (If in a hurry use cheese soup)

4 ounces crab meat, canned or packaged
1/4 cup celery, chopped
1/4 cup green pepper, chopped
1/4 cup onion, chopped
5 tablespoons mayonnaise, or more if needed

Cheese sauce:
2 tablespoons butter
2 tablespoons flour
1 tablespoon onion, grated
1 cup milk
1 cup cheddar cheese, grated
salt and pepper, to taste

Nutritional Values:
Per Serving (excluding unknown items): 249 Calories; 21g Fat (75.7% calories from fat); 10g Protein; 5g Carbohydrate; trace Dietary Fiber; 54mg Cholesterol; 302mg Sodium.
Points: 7

Substitute Values:
Per Serving (using substitute whole wheat bread, fat-free mayonnaise, skim milk, and fat-free cheddar cheese): 191 Calories; 4g Fat (17.3% calories from fat); 15g Protein; 26g Carbohydrate; 3g Dietary Fiber; 19mg Cholesterol; 618mg Sodium.
Points: 4

Delicious Pancakes

Melt 1 stick butter in skillet. In a mixing bowl, combine ½ C flour, ½ C milk, 2 eggs, delicately beaten, and just the smallest pinch of nutmeg. Blend briskly, pour into skillet and bake at 325° for 15 or 20 min. Sprinkle with sugar, return briefly to the oven while you get the paper and make coffee. Remove pancake and sprinkle with lemon juice and serve.

Servings: 4
Start to finish: 30 minutes

1 cup butter
1/2 cup flour
1/2 cup milk
2 eggs
pinch nutmeg
4 tablespoons confectioner's sugar, garnish
1 tablespoon lemon juice, garnish

Nutritional Values:
Per Serving (excluding unknown items): 317 Calories; 27g Fat (75.1% calories from fat); 6g Protein; 14g Carbohydrate; trace Dietary Fiber; 172mg Cholesterol; 284mg Sodium.
Points: 9

Substitute Values:
Per Serving (using substitute imitation margarine, sugar substitutes, and egg substitute and skim milk): 218 Calories; 11g Fat (48.1% calories from fat); 8g Protein; 20g Carbohydrate; trace Dietary Fiber; 1mg Cholesterol; 403mg Sodium.
Points: 5

Filbert Puff Pancake with Strawberries

Beat eggs lightly in mixing bowl. Add milk, flour and nutmeg and beat until blended. Batter may be a little lumpy. Melt butter in a 10 to 12 in. skillet with heat proof handle over medium heat, until butter begins to foam. Stir in filberts. Pour batter in hot skillet over filberts. Bake at 425° 15-20 min. or until pancake is puffed and golden brown. Sprinkle with lemon juice and return to oven for 2-3 min. Sprinkle with confectioners sugar and serve at once. Cut into wedges and serve at once. Cut into wedges and serve with strawberries topped with sour cream, if desired.

Servings: 8
Start to finish: 40 minutes

2 eggs
1/2 cup milk
1/2 cup all-purpose flour
dash nutmeg
1/2 cup filberts, sliced thick or
2oz. hazelnuts
lemon juice, of 1 lemon
2 tablespoons confectioner's sugar
1 pint fresh strawberries, sliced and
sweetened
8 tablespoons sour cream, optional

Nutritional Values:
Per Serving (excluding unknown items): 161 Calories; 10g Fat (56.8% calories from fat); 5g Protein; 13g Carbohydrate; 2g Dietary Fiber; 61mg Cholesterol; 33mg Sodium.
Points: 4

Substitute Values:
Per Serving (using substitute fat-free sour cream, sugar substitutes, and egg substitute and skim milk): 128 Calories; 6g Fat (38.9% calories from fat); 6g Protein; 14g Carbohydrate; 2g Dietary Fiber; 2mg Cholesterol; 68mg Sodium.
Points: 3

Mom's Hotcakes

In medium bowl add buttermilk and baking soda, let stand until mixture doubles. Beat eggs and add milk and mix. Beat in flour, salt, sugar and vanilla. Pour a small amount of oil on griddle and smooth around with paper towel. Repeat between each batch of hotcakes.

Servings: 8
Preparation Time: 1 hour
Start to finish: 1 hour 30 minutes

1 cup buttermilk
1 teaspoon baking soda
2 eggs, beaten
1 cup flour
1 dash salt
1 tablespoon sugar
1/2 teaspoon vanilla, if desired
2 tablespoons oil, or cooking spray

Nutritional Values:
Per Serving (excluding unknown items): 125 Calories; 5g Fat (37.1% calories from fat); 4g Protein; 15g Carbohydrate; trace Dietary Fiber; 54mg Cholesterol; 241mg Sodium.
Points: 3

Substitute Values:
Per Serving (using substitute Enova cooking oil, sugar substitutes, egg substitute and low fat buttermilk): 74 Calories; trace Fat (3.4% calories from fat); 4g Protein; 13g Carbohydrate; trace Dietary Fiber; trace Cholesterol; 237mg Sodium.
Points: 1

GOODIES

GOODIES

Carmel Custard

In heavy saucepan, 1/2 cup sugar. Add 2 T boiling water and let mixture caramelize. Pour immediately into a 6 C mold and swirl around so caramel reaches all parts of the bottom and halfway up sides.
In a bowl mix heavy cream, milk, eggs, vanilla, fresh orange juice, grated orange rind, dark rum and sugar.
Pour egg mixture into caramelized mold. Bake in a water bath at 325° for about 45min. Or until knife inserted comes clean. Chill overnight and un-mold. Serve with whipped cream flavored with Cointreau or Grand Marnier (optional).

Servings: 8
Preparation Time: 1 hour
Start to finish: 24 hours

1/2 cup sugar
2 tablespoons boiling water
3 cups heavy cream (whipping cream)
5 egg
2 teaspoons vanilla
1/2 cup fresh orange juice
1 tablespoon orange rind, grated
1/4 cup dark rum
3/4 cup sugar

Nutritional Values:
Per Serving (excluding unknown items): 502 Calories; 36g Fat (66.0% calories from fat); 6g Protein; 36g Carbohydrate; trace Dietary Fiber; 255mg Cholesterol; 78mg Sodium.
Points: 13

Substitute Values:
Per Serving (using substitute heavy cream substitute, sugar substitutes, and egg substitute): 242 Calories; 11g Fat (47.1% calories from fat); 9g Protein; 20g Carbohydrate; trace Dietary Fiber; 1mg Cholesterol; 480mg Sodium.
Points: 6

Lemon Bars

Preheat oven to 350°. Melt 1 cup butter in sauce pan and place in a 13"x9" pan and stir in 1/2 cup powdered sugar and 2 cups sifted flour. Press in bottom of pan. Bake 20 min. at 350°.

Beat eggs, sugar and lemon juice. Sift together flour, salt and baking powder. Stir into egg mixture. Pour over baked crust. Bake 25 min. at 350°. Sprinkle with powdered sugar.

Servings: 12
Yield: 12 bars
Preparation Time: 20 minutes
Start to finish: 1 hour 5 minutes

2 cups sifted flour
1/2 cup powdered sugar
1 cup butter

2 cups sugar
4 eggs
4 tablespoons lemon juice
4 tablespoons flour
1 teaspoon baking powder
1/2 teaspoon salt

Nutritional Values:
Per Serving (excluding unknown items): 467 Calories; 21g Fat (39.2% calories from fat); 5g Protein; 67g Carbohydrate; 1g Dietary Fiber; 134mg Cholesterol; 372mg Sodium
Points: 11

Substitute Values:
Per Serving (using substitute margarine imitation, sugar substitutes, and egg substitute): 244 Calories; 8g Fat (29.5% calories from fat); 6g Protein; 36g Carbohydrate; 1g Dietary Fiber; 0mg Cholesterol; 452mg Sodium.
Points: 5

Toffee Bars

1 3/4 cups all-purpose flour
1 cup sugar
1 cup butter
1 teaspoon vanilla, extract
1 egg, separated
1/2 cup walnuts, finely chopped
(optional)

Preheat oven to 275°. Grease 15 ½ x 10 ½ jelly roll pan. In to large bowl, measure all ingredients except egg whites and walnuts. Mix at medium speed, until well mixed. Pat evenly in pan. In cup with fork, beat egg white slightly, brush over top of dough and sprinkle with nuts. Bake 1 hour 10 min. or until golden. Immediately cut into 50 bars or so and remove from pan to cool on wire rack. Store in tightly covered container for at least 3 days before serving.

Nutritional Values:
Per Serving (excluding unknown items): 73 Calories; 5g Fat (54.7% calories from fat); 1g Protein; 8g Carbohydrate; trace Dietary Fiber; 14mg Cholesterol; 39mg Sodium.
Points: 2

Substitute Values:
Per Serving (using substitute imitation margarine): 57 Calories; 3g Fat (41.4% calories from fat); 1g Protein; 8g Carbohydrate; trace Dietary Fiber; 4mg Cholesterol; 46mg Sodium.
Points: 1

Servings: 50
Yield: 50 bars
Start to finish: 1:20 minutes

Fudge Brownies

In medium sauce pan melt butter and unsweetened chocolate. Remove from heat, stir in sugar. Blend in eggs one at a time. Add vanilla. Stir in flour nuts and chocolate chips, mix well. Spread in greased 8x8x2 pan. Bake 350° for 30 min. and test with toothpick . Cool before cutting into squares.

Servings: 12
Preparation Time: 15 minutes
Start to finish: 45 minutes

1/2 cup butter
1 cup sugar
1 teaspoon vanilla
2 eggs
2 ounces sifted all purpose flour
1/2 cup walnuts, chopped (optional)
4 ounces chocolate chips

Nutritional Values:
Per Serving (excluding unknown items): 175 Calories; 14g Fat (70.2% calories from fat); 3g Protein; 10g Carbohydrate; 1g Dietary Fiber; 56mg Cholesterol; 91mg Sodium.
Points: 4
Substitute Values:
Per Serving (using substitute omit nuts, sugar substitutes, egg substitute and margarine imitation): 137 Calories; 7g Fat (42.9% calories from fat); 3g Protein; 17g Carbohydrate; 1g Dietary Fiber; 0mg Cholesterol; 154mg Sodium.
Points: 3

Nutty Butter Balls

Mix butter, sugar, vanilla, and flour mix well. Add nuts and mix well. Chill about 20 min. shape into balls and place on un-greased cookie sheet. Bake at 350° 12-15 min. Roll in powdered sugar while warm.

Servings: 24
Yield: 1 dozen
Start to finish: 60 minutes

1 cup margarine
1/2 cup sugar
1 teaspoon vanilla
2 cups sifted all purpose flour
1 cup nuts, chopped

Nutritional Values:
Per Serving (excluding unknown items): 127 Calories; 9g Fat (59.3% calories from fat); 2g Protein; 11g Carbohydrate; 1g Dietary Fiber; 14mg Cholesterol; 53mg Sodium.
Points: 3

Substitute Values:
Per Serving (using substitute margarine and sugar): 115 Calories; 7g Fat (55.1% calories from fat); 2g Protein; 11g Carbohydrate; 1g Dietary Fiber; 0mg Cholesterol; 94mg Sodium.
Points: 3

Pumpkin Pudding Pleaser

Set 1 cup of yellow cake mix aside and pour rest in mixing bowl. Combine with melted butter and 1 beaten egg, blend well. Spread crust mixture in 9"x13" baking dish. In separate bowl beat 2 eggs, add pumpkin and milk. Blend and pour on unbaked crust. Take 1 cup of yellow cake mix cut in margarine, sugar and cinnamon into cake mix. Blend in pecans and sprinkle mixture over filling. Bake at 350° 1 hour 10min. Until knife comes out clean. Serve with whip cream on top.

Servings: 12
Preparation Time: 20 minutes
Start to finish: 1 hour 10 minutes

2 cups yellow cake mix
1/2 cup butter, melted
1 whole egg, beaten

Filling:
30 ounces pumpkin, canned
12 ounces evaporated milk, add water to make 2 cups
2 eggs

Topping:
1 cup cake mix
1/4 cup butter
1/2 cup sugar
1 teaspoon cinnamon
1 cup pecans, chopped (optional)

Nutritional Values:
Per Serving (excluding unknown items): 386 Calories; 24g Fat (54.0% calories from fat); 5g Protein; 41g Carbohydrate; 3g Dietary Fiber; 85mg Cholesterol; 416mg Sodium.
Points: 9

Substitute Values:
Per Serving (using substitute omit nuts, sugar substitutes, egg substitute and margarine imitation): 307 Calories; 11g Fat (31.1% calories from fat); 7g Protein; 46g Carbohydrate; 3g Dietary Fiber; 2mg Cholesterol; 512mg Sodium.
Points: 6

Cherry Dessert

Mix cake, eggs, butter. Spread un-greased pan 13x9x2. Spread pie filing over and sprinkle on nuts. Bake at 350° for 45 min. Cool about 15 min. While dessert is cooling combine confectioners sugar and water to glaze. Pour over dessert and serve.

Servings: 12
Preparation Time: 15 minutes
Start to finish: 1 hour

18 3/4 ounces cake mix, cherry chip packaged
2 eggs
1/2 cup butter
29 ounces cherry pie filling (2cans)
1 cup nuts, chopped
Glaze:
1 cup confectioner's sugar
1 tablespoon water

Nutritional Values:
Per Serving (excluding unknown items): 459 Calories; 20g Fat (38.4% calories from fat); 5g Protein; 67g Carbohydrate; 2g Dietary Fiber; 56mg Cholesterol; 391mg Sodium.
Points: 10

Substitute Values:
Per Serving (using substitute omit nuts, sugar substitutes, egg substitute and margarine imitation): 341 Calories; 9g Fat (22.9% calories from fat); 4g Protein; 62g Carbohydrate; 1g Dietary Fiber; 0mg Cholesterol; 453mg Sodium.
Points: 7

Pistachio Dessert

Mix flour, butter and pecans together and press into greased 9x13" pan. Bake at 350° for 30 min. or until done. Next cream together with mixer cream cheese, powdered sugar, and cool whip. Spread over pecan crust. Take instant pudding mix and 3 cups milk and beat. Pour over baked crust in pan. Let set for a few minutes. Spread rest of cool whip on top and refrigerate.

Servings: 10
Start to finish: 2:30 minutes

1 1/2 cups flour
1/2 cup butter
1 cup nuts, pecans chopped
8 ounces cream cheese
1 cup sifted powdered sugar
12 ounces cool whip , (1/2 container)
2 packages instant pudding mix, pistachio
3 cups milk

Nutritional Values:
Per Serving (excluding unknown items): 476 Calories; 28g Fat (51.5% calories from fat); 9g Protein; 50g Carbohydrate; 2g Dietary Fiber; 60mg Cholesterol; 495mg Sodium.
Points: 11

Substitute Values:
Per Serving (using substitute imitation margarine, sugar substitutes, milk substitute and fat free/sugar free instant pudding mix): 282 Calories; 13g Fat (41.8% calories from fat); 10g Protein; 31g Carbohydrate; 2g Dietary Fiber; 3mg Cholesterol; 313mg Sodium.
Points: 6

Tropic Torte

Sift together sugar, flour, baking soda , baking powder, and salt. Add 1 can fruit cocktail to which enough water has been added to make 2 cups, beaten egg and vanilla. Put in 8x12 buttered pan and sprinkle with brown sugar and chopped nuts. Bake at 325° for 50 min. for tin pan and for glass at 300°.

Servings: 6
Start to finish: 60 minutes

1 cup sugar
1 1/2 cups flour
1 teaspoon baking soda
1 teaspoon baking powder
1/4 teaspoon salt
1 cup brown sugar
1/2 cup nuts, chopped
15 ounces fruit cocktail in light syrup
1 egg, beaten
1 teaspoon vanilla
water

Nutritional Values:
Per Serving (excluding unknown items): 462 Calories; 8g Fat (14.9% calories from fat); 7g Protein; 94g Carbohydrate; 3g Dietary Fiber; 35mg Cholesterol; 407mg Sodium.
Points: 10

Substitute Values:
Per Serving (using using substitute omit nuts, sugar substitutes, egg substitute, carb clever fruit cocktail): 276 Calories; trace Fat (1.2% calories from fat); 5g Protein; 53g Carbohydrate; 1g Dietary Fiber; 0mg Cholesterol; 537mg Sodium.
Points: 5

Cold Sherry Souffle

Soften gelatin in ½ C cold water for 5 min. Place over boiling water and stir until dissolved. Remove from heat and add sherry. Cool. Chill for 30 minutes or until mixture begins to thicken. Meanwhile beat egg whites until foamy. Add ½ C sugar gradually, beating constantly. Add lemon juice and beat until mixture is stiff but not dry. Beat egg yolks until frothy, add ¼ C sugar gradually and beat until yolks are thick and lemon colored. Add slightly thickened wine gelatin slowly to egg yolks and continue beating until thick and light. Fold beaten egg whites into gelatin mixture. Whip cream and fold in. Pour into a collared 7 in. souffle dish lined with lady fingers. Chill for 3 hours or until firm. Remove paper collar before serving. Serve with additional whipped cream if desired.

To make collar for the souffle dish, cut a strip of waxed paper 6in. Wide and long enough to fit around the top of the dish. Fold over to make a double strip 3 in. wide. Butter on side and tie the strip around the dish, buttered side in, so that it stands like a collar above the edge.

Servings: 12
Start to finish: 4:00 hours

1 1/2 cups sweet sherry
6 eggs, separated
1 tablespoon lemon juice
3/4 cup sugar
2 envelopes unflavored gelatin
1 cup heavy cream
15 ladyfinger cookies

Nutritional Values:
Per Serving (excluding unknown items): 298 Calories; 11g Fat (36.9% calories from fat); 6g Protein; 36g Carbohydrate; trace Dietary Fiber; 183mg Cholesterol; 103mg Sodium.
Points: 7

Angel Food Cheese Dessert

Break up angel food cake into bite size pieces. Beat 8oz. Philadelphia cream cheese and add ½ C powdered sugar until fluffy. Add 1 C cool whip. Spread on cake until each piece is covered. Pat evenly in 9x13 pan. Pour 2 ½ can cherry pie filling over top. Refrigerate 24 hours. Cut in squares.

Servings: 12
Start to finish: 24 hours

1 angel cake, whole, broken up bite size pieces
8 ounces cream cheese
1/2 cup powdered sugar
1 cup Cool Whip®
29 ounces cherry pie filling (2 cans)

Nutritional Values:
Per Serving (excluding unknown items): 308 Calories; 8g Fat (22.6% calories from fat); 5g Protein; 56g Carbohydrate; 1g Dietary Fiber; 21mg Cholesterol; 316mg Sodium.
Points: 7

Substitute Values:
Per Serving (using fat free cream cheese, sugar substitutes, and sugar free cool whip): 241 Calories; 1g Fat (2.0% calories from fat); 6g Protein; 54g Carbohydrate; 1g Dietary Fiber; 2mg Cholesterol; 378mg Sodium.
Points: 5

New England Rum Cheese Cake

Combine buttermilk, sugar, graham crackers and cinnamon and form crust. Line pie tin (9in.) with crust. For filling mix together cream cheese, 1/2 c sugar, eggs and rum. Pour mixture in pie crust and bake 20 min. at 375°. Meanwhile prepare topping by combining 1/2 cup sour cream, 1 T sugar and 1 T rum, mix well. Spread on baked pie. Bake 5 min. more. Cool. Serve cold. Pie can be frozen.

Servings: 10
Start to finish: 40 minutes Cool or refrigerate for several hours before serving

1/4 pound Butter
1/3 C sugar
18 graham crackers
dash of cinnamon
1/3 cup sugar
18 graham crackers, crushed
dash cinnamon
32 ounces cream cheese
1/2 cup sugar
2 eggs, beaten moderately stiff
1 tablespoon rum, or 1 1/2 tsp rum flavoring
1/2 cup sour cream
1 tablespoon sugar
1 tablespoon rum

Nutritional Values:
Per Serving (excluding unknown items): 497 Calories; 45g Fat (82.3% calories from fat); 9g Protein; 13g Carbohydrate; trace Dietary Fiber; 172mg Cholesterol; 458mg Sodium.
Points: 13

Substitute Values:
Per Serving (using substitute sugar substitutes, and egg substitute, fat-free sour cream, and fat-free cream cheese): 238 Calories; 7g Fat (27.4% calories from fat); 17g Protein; 24g Carbohydrate; trace Dietary Fiber; 9mg Cholesterol; 757mg Sodium.
Points: 5

No Cook Pie

Whip the cream and fold other ingredients into whipped cream. Spread on Graham cracker crust and refrigerate for at least 2 hours before serving.

Servings: 8
Start to finish: 2:30 minutes

1/2 pint whipping cream
1 pint marshmallow whip
2 bananas, sliced
1 small can crushed pineapple, drained
1 cup chopped nuts
1 Graham cracker crust

Nutritional Values:
Per Serving (excluding unknown items): 322 Calories; 21g Fat (60.8% calories from fat); 8g Protein; 22g Carbohydrate; 1g Dietary Fiber; 147mg Cholesterol; 86mg Sodium.
Points: 8

Substitute Values:
Per Serving (using substitute light cream, sugar substitutes, and egg substitute and fat free cream cheese): 211 Calories; 9g Fat (41.5% calories from fat); 11g Protein; 17g Carbohydrate; 1g Dietary Fiber; 28mg Cholesterol; 344mg Sodium
Points: 5

Poppy Seed Cake

Combine all ingredients in large mixing bowl, stirring to blend. Beat at medium speed 5 min. Scraping sides of bowl frequently. Pour into 10" bundt pan. Bake at 350° for 1 hour. Cool in pan on rack about 15 min. Turn on cake plate. Cool before cutting.

Servings: 8
Start to finish: 2:00 hours

18 3/4 ounces Yellow cake mix
1 ounce instant French vanilla pudding
4 whole eggs
1 cup sour cream
1/2 cup cooking oil
1/2 cup sherry
1/3 cup poppy seeds (1 box)

Nutritional Values:
Per Serving (excluding unknown items): 571 Calories; 32g Fat (52.1% calories from fat); 8g Protein; 59g Carbohydrate; 1g Dietary Fiber; 120mg Cholesterol; 540mg Sodium.
Points: 14

Substitute Values:
Per Serving (using substitute Enova cooking oil, fat free sour cream, egg substitute and fat-free sugar-free instant pudding mix): 384 Calories; 10g Fat (25.3% calories from fat); 11g Protein; 59g Carbohydrate; 1g Dietary Fiber; 5mg Cholesterol; 545mg Sodium.
Points: 8

Pineapple Cheese Pie

Combine graham crackers, sugar and butter and reserve ¼ of the mixture for topping. Press remaining mixture in 9" pie pan. Blend cream cheese, 2 tablespoons butter, egg and set aside. Combine flour, milk and crushed pineapple and mix with cream cheese mixture. Pour into crumb crust and top with reserved graham cracker crumbs mixture. Bake at 350° for 35 min. Chill and serve.

Servings: 8
Start to finish: 60 minutes

1 1/4 cups graham cracker crumbs, or prepared graham pie crust
1/3 cup sugar
1/3 cup butter, melted
Reserve: ¼ of mixture for topping.

8 ounces creamed cheese , softened
2 tablespoons butter
1 whole egg
2 tablespoons flour
2/3 cup milk
9 ounces crushed pineapple, canned

Nutritional Values:
Per Serving (excluding unknown items): 229 Calories; 13g Fat (50.9% calories from fat); 3g Protein; 26g Carbohydrate; 1g Dietary Fiber; 58mg Cholesterol; 206mg Sodium.
Points: 8

Substitute Values:
Per Serving (using substitute fat free cream cheese, sugar substitutes, egg substitute and skim milk):   184 Calories; 7g Fat (34.0% calories from fat); 7g Protein; 23g Carbohydrate; 1g Dietary Fiber; 3mg Cholesterol; 410mg Sodium.
Points: 4

Dump Cake

Empty apples (pie filling) into large bowl. Break eggs over apples. Add sugar, oil, cinnamon, flour, salt, soda, and nuts. Stir with spoon and spread into greased 9x13" pan. Bake at 325° 1 hour. Serve warm or cold with whipped cream.

Servings: 10
Preparation Time: 20 minutes
Start to finish: 1 hour

1 ounce apple pie filling
2 whole egg
2 cups sugar
1/2 cup oil
2 teaspoons cinnamon
1 teaspoon vanilla
2 cups flour
1 teaspoon baking soda
1 cup walnuts, chopped
1/4 cup salt

Nutritional Values:
Per Serving (excluding unknown items): 438 Calories; 19g Fat (38.6% calories from fat); 7g Protein; 62g Carbohydrate; 2g Dietary Fiber; 42mg Cholesterol; 2700mg Sodium.
Points: 11

Substitute Values:
Per Serving (using substitute omit nuts, Enova cooking oil, sugar substitutes, and egg substitute): 184 Calories; trace Fat (1.8% calories from fat); 5g Protein; 38g Carbohydrate; 1g Dietary Fiber; 0mg Cholesterol; 2797mg Sodium.
Points: 3

Cherry Blintz Cake

Mix cake mix with 4 egg yolks, add 1 ½ C water. Divide batter evenly and pour into 2 9x13" pans. Beat egg whites to soft peaks (not dry). Add 2/3 C sugar. Spread egg white mixture on each pan of cake batter. Sprinkle with ¼ C sugar and slivered almonds. Bake at 350° for 25-30 min. Let cool. On one cake spread cherry pie filling and whipped cream. Place on first cake with almond side up.

Servings: 12
Start to finish: 40 minutes

18 3/4 ounces Yellow cake mix
1 pint heavy cream
30 ounces cherry pie filling (2 cans)
3 tablespoons slivered almonds
4 egg yolks, set aside whites
1 1/2 cups water
2/3 cup sugar

Nutritional Values:
Per Serving (excluding unknown items): 486 Calories; 23g Fat (41.5% calories from fat); 5g Protein; 68g Carbohydrate; 1g Dietary Fiber; 126mg Cholesterol; 316mg Sodium.
Points: 11

Substitute Values:
Per Serving (using substitute heavy cream substitute, and sugar substitutes): 382 Calories; 13g Fat (30.8% calories from fat); 5g Protein; 62g Carbohydrate; 1g Dietary Fiber; 72mg Cholesterol; 462mg Sodium.
Points: 9

Fresh Apple Cake

Combine all ingredients in mixing bowl. Pour into 9"x13" baking pan and bake at 350° for 45 to 50 min. Cool. Frost with cream cheese frosting. Scatter nuts on top (optional)

Servings: 12
Start to finish: 1:20 minutes

2 eggs
2 cups sugar
2 teaspoons baking soda
pinch salt
1/2 cup oil
1 cup nuts, chopped
2 teaspoons cinnamon
1 teaspoon vanilla
2 cups flour
4 cups apples, diced
Frosting:
3 teaspoons butter, softened
6 ounces cream cheese
1/2 cup powdered sugar
1 teaspoon vanilla

Nutritional Values:
Per Serving (excluding unknown items): 473 Calories; 23g Fat (42.5% calories from fat); 6g Protein; 63g Carbohydrate; 3g Dietary Fiber; 53mg Cholesterol; 275mg Sodium.
Points: 11

Substitute Values:
Per Serving (using substitute omit nuts, Enova cooking oil, sugar substitutes, fat free cream cheese and egg substitute): 211 Calories; 1g Fat (4.8% calories from fat); 6g Protein; 43g Carbohydrate; 2g Dietary Fiber; 1mg Cholesterol; 392mg Sodium.
Points: 4

Chocolate Fudge Cake

Sift flour and sugar together. Set aside. Combine oleo, cocoa, water and salad oil in 2 qt. Saucepan. Bring to boil, stirring constantly. Remove from heat and pour over flour and sugar. Mix well by hand. Add buttermilk, soda and eggs. Mix well again. Bake 20-25 min. at 400° in well greased and floured baking pan 13x9x2" (Pam flour spray works great). To frost combine all ingredients and spread on cooled cake.

Servings: 12
Start to finish: 60 minutes

2 cups flour
2 cups sugar
1/2 cup butter
4 tablespoons cocoa
1 cup water
1/2 cup oil
1/2 cup buttermilk
1 teaspoon baking soda
2 whole eggs, beaten well

Frosting:
1/2 cup butter
6 tablespoons buttermilk
4 tablespoons cocoa
16 ounces powdered sugar
1 cup nuts, chopped
1 teaspoon vanilla

Nutritional Values:
Per Serving (excluding unknown items): 669 Calories; 33g Fat (42.7% calories from fat); 7g Protein; 92g Carbohydrate; 3g Dietary Fiber; 77mg Cholesterol; 295mg Sodium.
Points: 16

Substitute Values:
Per Serving (using substitute omit nuts, Enova cooking oil, sugar substitutes, egg substitute, buttermilk substitute-plain yogurt and): 383 Calories; 9g Fat (20.8% calories from fat); 5g Protein; 71g Carbohydrate; 2g Dietary Fiber; 2mg Cholesterol; 393mg Sodium.
Points: 8

Mayonnaise Cake

Beat all at once in mixer. Bake at 350° for 35 min. or until done. (This is a moist chocolate cake – so easy). Frost with favorite frosting.

Servings: 10
Start to finish: 45 minutes

2 cups flour
1 cup sugar
5 tablespoons cocoa
2 teaspoons baking soda
1 cup mayonnaise
1 cup water
1 teaspoon vanilla

Nutritional Values:
Per Serving (excluding unknown items): 334 Calories; 19g Fat (49.7% calories from fat); 3g Protein; 41g Carbohydrate; 2g Dietary Fiber; 8mg Cholesterol; 379mg Sodium.
Points: 8

Substitute Values:
Per Serving (using substitute fat free mayonnaise, and sugar substitutes): 156 Calories; 1g Fat (3.6% calories from fat); 3g Protein; 34g Carbohydrate; 2g Dietary Fiber; 0mg Cholesterol; 596mg Sodium.
Points: 3

Pumpkin Pecan Bundt Cake

Preheat oven 350°. Grease bundt pan with butter, sprinkle with flour. Combine all ingredients and beat at medium speed 5 min. Add ½ C pecans. Reserve whole pecans for side of cake. Place whole pecans in bottom of pan. Pour in batter and bake at 350° 40-50 min. Serve with whipped cream.

Servings: 12
Start to finish: 60 minutes

18 3/4 ounces spice cake mix
1 cup canned pumpkin
1/2 cup oil
3 3/8 ounces instant vanilla pudding and pie filling
3 eggs
1 teaspoon cinnamon
1/2 cup water

Nutritional Values:
Per Serving (excluding unknown items): 306 Calories; 16g Fat (45.6% calories from fat); 4g Protein; 38g Carbohydrate; 1g Dietary Fiber; 54mg Cholesterol; 333mg Sodium.
Points: 7

Substitute Values:
Per Serving (using substitute Enova cooking oil, fat free sugar free instant pudding, and egg substitute): 241 Calories; 5g Fat (19.6% calories from fat); 5g Protein; 44g Carbohydrate; 1g Dietary Fiber; 1mg Cholesterol; 447mg Sodium.
Points: 5

Carrot Cake

Mix together 2 cups sugar , 4 eggs and 1 ¼ oil. Then add to mixture flour, baking soda, baking powder, cinnamon and salt. Mix in carrots, walnuts (optional), and pineapple. Pour into baking sheet or 3-9"cake pans and bake at 350° for 60 min. after cake cools frost with icing. Mix together cream cheese, powdered sugar, butter and vanilla and beat until creamy.

Servings: 12
Start to finish: 1:20 minutes

2 cups sugar
4 eggs
1 1/4 cups oil
2 cups flour
2 teaspoons baking powder
1 1/2 teaspoons baking soda
3 teaspoons cinnamon
1 teaspoon salt
1 1/2 cups walnuts
2 cups grated carrots
8 ounces crushed pineapple, drained

Icing:
8 ounces cream cheese
16 ounces powdered sugar
1/2 cup butter
1 1/2 teaspoons vanilla

Nutritional Values:
Per Serving (excluding unknown items): 829 Calories; 48g Fat (50.6% calories from fat); 10g Protein; 95g Carbohydrate; 2g Dietary Fiber; 112mg Cholesterol; 582mg Sodium.
Points: 20

Substitute Values:
Per Serving (using substitute omit nuts, Enova cooking oil, sugar substitutes, egg substitute and fat free cream cheese): 379 Calories; 4g Fat (10.5% calories from fat); 8g Protein; 75g Carbohydrate; 2g Dietary Fiber; 2mg Cholesterol; 741mg Sodium.
Points: 8

Rainbow Cake

Combine separately Lime, Cherry, and orange jell-o in three 8x8" pans, using 1 C hot water and ½ C cold water. Chill then cut into cubes.

Line a 9" spring form cake pan with lady fingers (2 pkg.) or use a graham cracker crust on bottom and sides.

Dissolve 1 lemon jell-o in 1 C of heated pineapple juice with ¼ C sugar added. Add ½ C cold water. Chill until syrupy. Whip 2 C whipping cream and fold into syrupy lemon jello.

Add syrupy lemon jell-o to the first three jell-o's which have been cut into small cubes. Fold gently.

Pour into lined 9" spring form cake pan and refrigerate 8 hours.

Servings: 12
Preparation Time: 30 minutes
Start to finish: 8 hours

6 ounces lime jello
6 ounces orange jell-o
6 ounces cherry jell-o
6 ounces lemon jell-o
10 1/2 ounces lady fingers
(2 pkg by Milano)
hot water
cold water
1 cup pineapple juice, heated
2 cups heavy cream
1/4 cup sugar

Nutritional Values:
Per Serving (excluding unknown items): 165 Calories; 15g Fat (78.6% calories from fat); 1g Protein; 8g Carbohydrate; trace Dietary Fiber; 54mg Cholesterol; 15mg Sodium.
Points: 4

Substitute Values:
Per Serving (using substitute fat and sugar free Jell-o's, sugar substitutes, and light cream): 169 Calories; 8g Fat (45.1% calories from fat); 3g Protein; 20g Carbohydrate; trace Dietary Fiber; 113mg Cholesterol; 52mg Sodium.
Points: 4

Strawberry Pie

Cook in saucepan. Bring to a boil, put in refrigerator until slightly thickened. Remove and fold in 1 C cool whip and 1 C strawberries. Put in a graham cracker pie shell. Cover with Cool Whip and arrange strawberries on top. Keep refrigerated.

Servings: 8
Serving size: ½ Cup
Start to finish: 2 hours refrigerated

1/16 ounce vanilla pudding mix
6 ounces strawberry jello
1 cup water
1 teaspoon lemon juice
1 graham cracker crumb pie crust
1 cup strawberries
1 cup Cool Whip®

Nutritional Values:
Per Serving (excluding unknown items): 179 Calories; 9g Fat (45.5% calories from fat); 1g Protein; 23g Carbohydrate; 1g Dietary Fiber; 0mg Cholesterol; 175mg Sodium.
Points: 4

Substitute Values:
Per Serving : 153 Calories; 8g Fat (43.2% calories from fat); 1g Protein; 21g Carbohydrate; 1g Dietary Fiber; 0mg Cholesterol; 172mg Sodium.
Points: 4

Lemon Pie

Mix together first 5 ingredients until smooth, add water and cook until thick. Pour into baked pie shell and top with meringue. For Meringue: Beat eggs whites, add a pinch of salt and cream of tarter. Gradually add and beat well 6 T sugar. Add vanilla and lemon juice. Bake at 425° about 8-10 min.

Servings: 8
Start to finish: 60 minutes

1 whole Lemon (grated rind and juice)
3 egg yolks, set aside whites
1 cup sugar
1 tablespoon butter
3 tablespoons flour
1 cup boiling water
pinch salt
1 pie shell, cooked

Meringue:
3 egg whites
pinch salt
1 teaspoon cream of tarter, or more if needed
6 tablespoons sugar
1/2 teaspoon vanilla

Nutritional Values:
Per Serving (excluding unknown items): 287 Calories; 9g Fat (29.2% calories from fat); 4g Protein; 48g Carbohydrate; 1g Dietary Fiber; 84mg Cholesterol; 185mg Sodium.
Points: 6

Substitute Values:
Per Serving (using sugar substitutes): 214 Calories; 9g Fat (37.8% calories from fat); 4g Protein; 28g Carbohydrate; 1g Dietary Fiber; 80mg Cholesterol; 254mg Sodium.
Points: 6

Yogurt Pie

In large bowl combine cream, yogurt and fruit, mixing well. Spoon into pie shell and chill for at least three hours.

Servings: 8
Start to finish: 3 hours

1 graham cracker crumb pie crust
8 ounces heavy cream
8 ounces raspberry yogurt , or any flavor
12 ounces red raspberries, frozen, or match your yogurt flavor

Nutritional Values:
Per Serving (excluding unknown items): 289 Calories; 18g Fat (54.7% calories from fat); 2g Protein; 31g Carbohydrate; 2g Dietary Fiber; 39mg Cholesterol; 182mg Sodium.
Points: 7

Substitute Values:
Per Serving (using fat free cool whip and fat free yogurt): 212 Calories; 8g Fat (34.5% calories from fat); 2g Protein; 31g Carbohydrate; 2g Dietary Fiber; trace Cholesterol; 189mg Sodium.
Points: 5

Ice Box Lemon Pie

Combine vanilla wafers and butter and mold into pie shell. In double boiler mix egg yolks, sugar, lemon juice, grated rind and cream. Cook until thick. Cool. Fold in 3 egg whites, beaten stiff and 1 C heavy cream, whipped. Pour into crust. Freeze overnight or until firm. Let stand in refrigerator 20 min. before serving.

Servings: 8
Start to finish: 3 hours

Notes: A double boiler is a specialized piece of kitchen equipment consisting of two fitted saucepans. The larger saucepan is partially filled with water brought to a simmer or boil. The inner saucepan uses this indirect heat to melt chocolate, cook custards and sauces.

Crust:
1 1/4 cups vanilla wafers, crumbled
1/4 cup butter

Filling:
3 egg yolks
1/4 cup lemon juice
grated lemon rind
1 cup heavy cream, whipped

Nutritional Values:
Per Serving (excluding unknown items): 352 Calories; 26g Fat (65.1% calories from fat); 3g Protein; 28g Carbohydrate; 1g Dietary Fiber; 136mg Cholesterol; 186mg Sodium.
Points: 9

Substitute Values:
Per Serving (using substitute light cream): 268 Calories; 17g Fat (55.0% calories from fat); 3g Protein; 27g Carbohydrate; 1g Dietary Fiber; 96mg Cholesterol; 191mg Sodium.
Points: 7

Crème de Menthe Chocolate Pie

Cream butter and sugar; blend in chocolate and cream de' menthe. Add eggs one at a time; beat 5 min. after each addition. Add gelatin melted in water. Pour mixture into baked pie shell. Refrigerate 2 hours and top with whipped cream.

Servings: 8
Start to finish: 1:20 minutes

1/2 cup butter
3/4 cup sugar
1 square melted chocolate
1 envelope gelatin
2 eggs
1/4 cup water
2-3 tsp creame de menthe
1 pie shell, baked

Nutritional Values:
Per Serving (excluding unknown items): 385 Calories; 24g Fat (55.0% calories from fat); 4g Protein; 41g Carbohydrate; 1g Dietary Fiber; 84mg Cholesterol; 290mg Sodium.
Points: 10

Substitute Values:
Per Serving (using substitute sugar substitutes, and egg substitute): 291 Calories; 17g Fat (52.3% calories from fat); 5g Protein; 31g Carbohydrate; 1g Dietary Fiber; 0mg Cholesterol; 373mg Sodium.
Points: 7

Mother's Pumpkin Pie

Beat together pumpkin, sugar, flour, cinnamon, cloves, ginger, eggs. Fill pumpkin can full of milk and add to pumpkin mixture. Stir well. Add one tsp lemon extract and stir. Pour into unbaked crusts and bake at 325°oven 1 hour. Reduce heat when crusts have browned. The lemon extract is the secret of pies like mother makes.

Servings: 24
Yield: 3 pies
Preparation Time: 20 minutes
Start to finish: 1 hour

30 ounces canned pumpkin (fill empty can with milk and set aside)
2 cups sugar
3 tablespoons flour, heaping
1 teaspoon cinnamon
1/4 teaspoon cloves, ground
2 teaspoons ginger
3 eggs, large
1 teaspoon lemon extract
3 pie crusts unbaked

Nutritional Values:
Per Serving (excluding unknown items): 126 Calories; 7g Fat (48.1% calories from fat); 3g Protein; 14g Carbohydrate; 2g Dietary Fiber; 27mg Cholesterol; 156mg Sodium.
Points: 3

Substitute Values:
Per Serving (using substitute sugar substitutes, and egg substitute): 155 Calories; 6g Fat (36.4% calories from fat); 3g Protein; 21g Carbohydrate; 2g Dietary Fiber; 0mg Cholesterol; 201mg Sodium.
Points: 3

Fried Apricot Pies

(Substitute other fruit)

Cover 1 lb. Dried apricots with water and simmer until done. Mash, add sugar to taste. Continue to let cook until thick. Put aside and let cool.

Make pie crust with 2 c flour and 1/3 c oil; mix like as coarse meal. Add cold milk – 5 or 6 T. Make dough a little wetter than regular pie dough. Pinch off enough dough to roll into 3 in. diameter and put only about 2 T apricot mixture in center. Fold the dough over and press around edges with fork. Turn and press other side. Tightly seal. Brown in medium hot oil on both sides. Place on absorbent paper and sprinkle them with sugar.

Servings: 16
Start to finish: 60 minutes

1 pound dried apricots
1/2 cup sugar, to taste
2 cups flour
1/3 cup oil
6 tablespoons milk
confectioner's sugar, to coat

Nutritional Values:
Per Serving (excluding unknown items): 192 Calories; 5g Fat (22.5% calories from fat); 3g Protein; 36g Carbohydrate; 3g Dietary Fiber; 1mg Cholesterol; 6mg Sodium.
Points: 4

Substitute Values:
Per Serving (using substitute Enova cooking oil, and sugar substitutes): 140 Calories; 1g Fat (3.3% calories from fat); 3g Protein; 32g Carbohydrate; 3g Dietary Fiber; 1mg Cholesterol; 18mg Sodium.
Points: 2

Potato Chip Cookies

Cream together sugar and butter. Then add to sugar mixture potato chips, vanilla, flour and nuts. Drop dough by tsp on greased cookie sheet. Press flat with fork dipped in ice water. Bake at 325° for 20 min. till light brown. Sprinkle with powdered or granulated sugar.

Servings: 40
Yield: 3 1/2 dozen
Start to finish: 1:10 minutes

1 cup butter
1/2 cup sugar
1 cup potato chips, crushed but not to fine
3/4 teaspoon vanilla
1 1/2 cups flour
1/2 cup nuts, chopped (optional)

Nutritional Values:
Per Serving (excluding unknown items): 110 Calories; 8g Fat (61.5% calories from fat); 1g Protein; 10g Carbohydrate; 1g Dietary Fiber; 12mg Cholesterol; 82mg Sodium.
Points: 3

Substitute Values:
Per Serving (using substitute omit nuts, sugar substitutes, and margarine imitation): 74 Calories; 4g Fat (52.8% calories from fat); 1g Protein; 8g Carbohydrate; trace Dietary Fiber; 0mg Cholesterol; 96mg Sodium.
Points: 2

Oatmeal-Molasses Cookies

(a delicious spicy cookie)

Stir together into mixing bowl, flour, sugar, soda, salt, ginger, and cloves. Add shortening, egg and molasses. Beat until smooth. Stir in oatmeal. Teaspoon batter onto ungreased cookie sheet. Bake at 375° for 10 to 11 min. Allow to cool a few minutes before removing from cookie sheet.

3 Dozen
Servings: 8
Start to finish: 1:20 minutes

1 1/2 cups all purpose flour
1 cup sugar
1 teaspoon baking soda
1/2 teaspoon salt
1 teaspoon ground ginger
¼ teaspoon ground cloves
1/2 cup shortening
1 egg
1/2 cup molasses
¾ cup quick cooking rolled oats

Nutritional Values:
Per Serving (excluding unknown items): 93 Calories; 3g Fat (31.3% calories from fat); 1g Protein; 15g Carbohydrate; trace Dietary Fiber; 6mg Cholesterol; 68mg Sodium.
Points: 2

Substitute Values:
Per Serving (using sugar substitutes): 82 Calories; 3g Fat (36.2% calories from fat); 1g Protein; 12g Carbohydrate; trace Dietary Fiber; 6mg Cholesterol; 79mg Sodium.
Points: 2

Lace Roll-Ups

1/2 cup butter
1/2 cup light corn syrup
2/3 cup brown sugar
1 cup flour, 1/2" cubes
1 cup nuts, chopped

Bring butter, sugar and syrup to boil in heavy saucepan (medium heat, stir constantly). Remove from heat, stir in flour and then nuts. Blend well. Drop batter (teaspoonful) about 3 in. apart on lightly buttered cookie sheet. Bake only 4 at a time. Bake at 375° for 5-6 min. Let stand 2 min. and loosen with spatula. Roll and store in tin container to keep crisp.

Nutritional Values:
Per Serving (excluding unknown items): 124 Calories; 7g Fat (50.4% calories from fat); 2g Protein; 14g Carbohydrate; 1g Dietary Fiber; 10mg Cholesterol; 50mg Sodium.
Points: 3

Servings: 24
Yield: 2 dozen
Start to finish: 30 minutes

Family Jewels

Combine in a large bowl candied cherries, candied pineapple, nuts, coconut, and butterscotch morsels. In separate bowl mix together flour, baking powder, baking soda and salt. Sift over fruit mixture, stirring gently until all the fruit is coated. Then mix together eggs, melted butter milk, brown sugar and vanilla. Pour over fruit mixture and mix gently until all the mixture is moistened. Drop by tablespoons on greased cookie sheet. Shape into the mounds with fingertip. Bake at 325° until medium brown for 15-20 min. Remove from cookie sheet at once and cool on wax paper. Put in covered container and let mellow several days.

Servings: 40
Preparation Time: 20 minutes
Start to finish: 1 hour

1/2 cup candied cherries, red
1/2 cup candied cherries, green
1 cup candied pineapple
2 cups walnuts
3 1/2 ounces coconut
6 ounces butterscotch morsels
3/4 cup flour
1/2 teaspoon baking powder
1/2 teaspoon baking soda
1/4 teaspoon salt
2 eggs, large
2 tablespoons butter, melted
1/4 cup milk
1/4 cup firmly packed brown sugar
2 teaspoons vanilla

Nutritional Values:
Per Serving (excluding unknown items): 95 Calories; 5g Fat (49.3% calories from fat); 2g Protein; 10g Carbohydrate; 1g Dietary Fiber; 13mg Cholesterol; 51mg Sodium.
Points: 2

Substitute Values:
Per Serving (using substitute omit nuts, sugar substitutes, skim milk, and egg substitute): 60 Calories; 2g Fat (27.0% calories from fat); 1g Protein; 9g Carbohydrate; trace Dietary Fiber; 2mg Cholesterol; 59mg Sodium.
Points: 1

Golden Pecan Tassie's

Preheat oven 350°. Blend butter and cheese, gradually add flour, mixing thoroughly. Chill dough. Take small pieces of dough and press in bottom and a little way up the sides of paper baking cups. Fill dough with pecan filling to edges of dough. Bake at 350° for 15 min. Reduce heat to 250° and bake 10 minutes longer. cool before serving.

Servings: 24
Preparation Time: 20 minutes
Start to finish: 30 minutes

1 cup butter
6 ounces cream cheese
2 cups flour
Pecan Filling:
2 eggs
1 1/2 cups brown sugar
2 tablespoons butter, melted
dash salt
1/2 teaspoon vanilla
1 cup pecans, coarsely chopped

Nutritional Values:
Per Serving (excluding unknown items): 209 Calories; 15g Fat (61.8% calories from fat); 3g Protein; 18g Carbohydrate; 1g Dietary Fiber; 49mg Cholesterol; 118mg Sodium.
Points: 5

Substitute Values:
Per Serving (using substitute fat free cream cheese, sugar substitutes, margarine imitation, and egg substitute): 193 Calories; 8g Fat (59.0% calories from fat); 3g Protein; 9g Carbohydrate; 1g Dietary Fiber; 18mg Cholesterol; 149mg Sodium.
Points: 4

Mother's Sugar Cookies

Cream butter and 2 c sugar with sugar, salt and vanilla. Add beaten eggs. Sift flour and baking powder together. Add to creamed mixture. Chill dough till firm enough to roll out on floured pastry cloth or board. Roll a little sugar in on top of dough. Cut with biscuit cutter. Bake at 425° till brown on greased and floured cookie sheet.

Servings: 36
Yield: 3 dozen
Preparation Time: 30 minutes
Start to finish: 1 hour

1 cup butter
2 cups sugar
2/3 teaspoon baking soda
1/2 teaspoon salt
1 teaspoon vanilla
3 eggs, beaten
3 1/2 cups sifted all purpose flour
2 teaspoons baking powder
powdered sugar

Nutritional Values:
Per Serving (excluding unknown items): 136 Calories; 6g Fat (37.1% calories from fat); 2g Protein; 20g Carbohydrate; trace Dietary Fiber; 31mg Cholesterol; 138mg Sodium.
Points: 3

Substitute Values:
Per Serving (using substitute Enova cooking oil, sugar substitutes, and egg substitute): 91 Calories; 3g Fat (30.9% calories from fat); 2g Protein; 13g Carbohydrate; trace Dietary Fiber; 18mg Cholesterol; 169mg Sodium.
Points: 2

Oatmeal Refrigerator Cookies

Cream together sugar, brown sugar and shortening. Beat eggs and vanilla well and add to sugar mixture. .Sift together flour, baking soda and salt and add quick oats and walnuts. Combine with sugar mixture and shape into rolls with waxed paper and refrigerate overnight. Preheat oven to 350°. Slice ¼ in. thick slices and bake for 10min.

Servings: 24
Yield: 2 dozen
Preparation Time: 30 minutes
Start to finish: 24 hours

1 cup sugar
1 cup brown sugar
1 cup shortening
2 egg
2 teaspoons vanilla
1 1/2 cups flour
1 teaspoon baking soda
1 teaspoon salt
2 cups quick cooking oats
1/2 cup walnuts

Nutritional Values:
Per Serving (excluding unknown items): 208 Calories; 11g Fat (46.6% calories from fat); 3g Protein; 25g Carbohydrate; 1g Dietary Fiber; 18mg Cholesterol; 150mg Sodium.
Points: 5

Substitute Values:
Per Serving (using substitute omit nuts, sugar substitutes): 202 Calories; 9g Fat (56.1% calories from fat); 2g Protein; 14g Carbohydrate; 1g Dietary Fiber; 18mg Cholesterol; 164mg Sodium.
Points: 5

Coconut Chews

Preheat oven to 350°. Cream shortening and confectioners' sugar. Blend in 1 ½ cup flour. Press evenly in bottom of un-greased baking pan, 13x9x2" and bake 12-15 min. Mix eggs, brown sugar, 2 tablespoons flour, salt, vanilla, coconut and walnuts and spread over hot baked layer and bake 20 minutes longer. Cool. Cut into bars about 3x1".

Orange Lemon Icing:
Mix 1 ½ cup confectioners sugar, 2 T butter or margarine, melted, 3 tablespoons orange juice and 1 tsp lemon juice. Mix the above until smooth and of spreading consistency. Spread over the cookie sheet while it is warm.

Servings: 36
Yield: 3 dozen
Preparation Time: 30 minutes
Start to finish: 1 hour

3/4 cup shortening (half butter softened)
3/4 cup confectioner's sugar
1 1/2 cups flour
2 whole eggs
1 cup brown sugar
2 tablespoons flour
1/2 teaspoon salt
1/2 teaspoon vanilla
1/2 cup coconut, flaked
1/2 cup walnuts
1/2 cup confectioner's sugar
Icing:
1 1/2 cups confectioner's sugar
2 tablespoons butter, melted
3 tablespoons orange juice
1 tablespoon lemon juice

Nutritional Values:
Per Serving (excluding unknown items): 134 Calories; 7g Fat (49.1% calories from fat); 2g Protein; 16g Carbohydrate; trace Dietary Fiber; 15mg Cholesterol; 46mg Sodium.
Points: 3

Substitute Values:
Per Serving (using substitute no shortening, margarine imitation, sugar substitutes, and egg substitute): 132 Calories; 3g Fat (30.6% calories from fat); 1g Protein; 16g Carbohydrate; trace Dietary Fiber; 13mg Cholesterol; 99mg Sodium.
Points: 3

Casey Jones Bars

Blend together brown sugar and butter. Then add flour baking powder and salt. Beat eggs and stir in coconut and chopped nuts. Put into 9"x13" cake pan. Bake for 25 to 30 minutes depending on your oven at 325°. Cool. Frost with butter and brown sugar by mixing in sauce pan until melted. Add 4 tablespoons milk, bring to boil and cool. Beat in 1 ½ cup powdered sugar. Spread on baked cake. Cut into squares.

Servings: 12
Yield: 12 squares
Preparation Time: 30 minutes
Start to finish: 30 minutes

2 cups brown sugar
1/2 cup butter
1 cup flour
2 teaspoons baking powder
1/2 teaspoon salt
2 eggs
2 cups coconut
1 cup nuts, chopped

Frosting:
6 tablespoons butter
1 cup brown sugar
4 tablespoons milk
1 1/2 cups powdered sugar

Nutritional Values:
Per Serving (excluding unknown items): 487 Calories; 26g Fat (45.9% calories from fat); 5g Protein; 63g Carbohydrate; 3g Dietary Fiber; 72mg Cholesterol; 339mg Sodium. Exchanges: 1/2 Grain(Starch); 1/2 Lean Meat; 0 Fruit; 0 Non-Fat Milk; 5 Fat; 3 1/2 Other Carbohydrates.
Points: 11

Substitute Values:
Per Serving (using substitute skim milk, margarine imitation, sugar substitutes, and egg substitute): 512 Calories; 12g Fat (48.8% calories from fat); 3g Protein; 25g Carbohydrate; 2g Dietary Fiber; 35mg Cholesterol; 350mg Sodium.
Points: 11

Josie's Brownies

Preheat oven 325°. Cream sugar and butter and add eggs, milk, vanilla, cake flour, baking powder, chocolate squares, salt and nuts in order given. Pour mixture and bake in 9x9" pan or baking dish at 325° for 25 min. Boil frosting until a soft ball forms in cold water. Beat frosting until thick enough to spread. Spread on brownies. Cool and cut into squares.

Servings: 9
Yield: 9 squares
Preparation Time: 30 minutes
Start to finish: 45 minutes

1 cup sugar
1/4 cup margarine
2 eggs, beaten
1/4 cup milk
1 teaspoon vanilla
1 cup cake flour
1/4 teaspoon baking powder
2 square chocolate, melted
1/4 teaspoon salt
1/2 cup , chopped

Frost with following :
1 cup sugar
1/3 cup milk
1 square chocolate
dash salt
1 teaspoon vanilla
1 tablespoon margarine

Nutritional Values:
Per Serving (excluding unknown items): 312 Calories; 16g Fat (44.3% calories from fat); 5g Protein; 40g Carbohydrate; 1g Dietary Fiber; 67mg Cholesterol; 164mg Sodium. Exchanges: 1 Grain(Starch); 1/2 Lean Meat; 0 Non-Fat Milk; 3 Fat; 2 Other Carbohydrates.
Points: 7

Substitute Values:
Per Serving (using substitute Enova cooking oil, sugar substitutes, and egg substitute): 230 Calories; 8g Fat (30.6% calories from fat); 3g Protein; 35g Carbohydrate; 1g Dietary Fiber; 47mg Cholesterol; 261mg Sodium.
Points: 5

Lemon Nut Bars

Mix as pie crust, ¾ cup butter and 1 ½ cup flour. Pat into 9x13" pan and bake 15min. at 325°. (If hard to handle, cool in freezer for a few minutes). Beat 3 eggs. Add 2 ¼ cups brown sugar, gradually and 1 tsp vanilla. Mix 3 T flour, ½ tsp salt, 1 cup chopped nuts and ½ tsp baking powder, add to egg mixture. Pour over the baked layer. Bake at 325° for 25 to 30 minutes. Cool.

Servings: 12
Start to finish: 60 minutes

3/4 cup butter
1 1/2 cups brown sugar
3 eggs
2 1/2 cups brown sugar
2 teaspoons vanilla
3 tablespoons flour
1/2 teaspoons salt
1 cup chopped nuts
1/2 teaspoon baking powder
2 1/2 cups powdered sugar
2 tablespoons butter
3 tablespoons orange juice
3 tablespoons lemon juice

Frosting: Beat until smooth and pour over bars.
2 ½ cups powdered sugar
2 tablespoons butter
3 tablespoons orange juice
3 tablespoons lemon juice

Nutritional Values:
Per Serving (excluding unknown items): 501 Calories; 21g Fat (37.3% calories from fat); 4g Protein; 77g Carbohydrate; 1g Dietary Fiber; 89mg Cholesterol; 284mg Sodium.
Points: 12

Substitute Values:
Per Serving (using substitute margarine, sugar substitutes, and egg substitute): 647 Calories; 13g Fat (46.0% calories from fat); 5g Protein; 30g Carbohydrate; 1g Dietary Fiber; 0mg Cholesterol; 316mg Sodium.
Points: 12

Pistachio Pudding Bars

Cream butter and sugar; add flour slowly. Add nuts. If mixture is too dry add a little more butter. Put in 9x13" baking pan. "Press" dough evenly in pan. Bake at 350° about 20-30 min. until light golden brown and cool.

1st Filling: Cream together 1 8oz. Pkg. Cream cheese and ½ C powdered sugar. Add about ¾ carton (9oz size) Cool Whip. Spread over cooled crust evenly.

2nd Filling: Mix 2 pkg. Pistachio instant pudding into 2 ½ C cold milk, stirring until pudding starts to thicken. Pour over first filling and spread evenly. Top this with more Cool Whip, about ½ to ¾ 9oz. Size carton. Garnish top with more chopped walnuts. Put in freezer. Before serving thaw slightly and cut medium small pieces.

Servings: 20
Start to finish: 60 minutes

Crust:
2 cups flour
4 tablespoons sugar
1/2 cup margarine
2/3 cup nuts, chopped
8 ounces cream cheese
1/2 cup powdered sugar
9 ounces cool whip
8 ounces Pistachio instant pudding

Nutritional Values:
Per Serving (excluding unknown items): 194 Calories; 12g Fat (57.4% calories from fat); 3g Protein; 18g Carbohydrate; 1g Dietary Fiber; 25mg Cholesterol; 83mg Sodium.
Points: 5

Substitute Values:
Per Serving (using omit nuts, sugar substitutes, and egg substitute, fat-free cream cheese, and Pistachio instant pudding fat free): 93 Calories; 3g Fat (24.8% calories from fat); 3g Protein; 14g Carbohydrate; trace Dietary Fiber; 1mg Cholesterol; 123mg Sodium.
Points: 2

Pumpkin Roll

Heat oven to 350°. Beat eggs 5 min. on high speed; gradually add sugar. Stir in pumpkin and lemon juice. Mix together flour, baking powder, cinnamon, ginger, nutmeg and salt. ; fold into pumpkin mix. Spread on greased and floured 15x10x1" cookie sheet. Top with nuts. Bake for 15min. Turn out on cheese cloth that has been sprinkled with powdered sugar. Starting at narrow end, roll up. When cool, unwrap.

Filling:
Combine 1 C powdered sugar, 2 3oz. Pkg. Cream cheese, 4 T butter and ½ tsp vanilla. Beat until smooth. Spread filling on cake; roll up. Let chill 1 hour. Slice and serve.

Servings: 10
Preparation Time: 30 minutes
Start to finish: 1 hour

3 eggs
1 cup sugar
2/3 cup pumpkin
1 teaspoon lemon juice
3/4 cup flour
1 teaspoon baking powder
2 teaspoons cinnamon
1 teaspoon ginger
1/2 teaspoon nutmeg
1/2 teaspoon salt
1 cup chopped nuts, finely chopped
Filling:
1 cup powdered sugar
6 ounces cream cheese
4 tablespoons butter
1/2 teaspoon vanilla

Nutritional Values:
Per Serving (excluding unknown items): 373 Calories; 20g Fat (47.3% calories from fat); 7g Protein; 44g Carbohydrate; 2g Dietary Fiber; 95mg Cholesterol; 276mg Sodium.
Points: 9

Substitute Values:
Per Serving (using omit nuts, sugar substitutes, and egg substitute, fat-free cream cheese, and margarine): 176 Calories; 3g Fat (13.9% calories from fat); 6g Protein; 31g Carbohydrate; 1g Dietary Fiber; 1mg Cholesterol; 394mg Sodium..
Points: 4

Overnight Coffee cake

Cream together granulated sugar, brown sugar and margarine. The add flour, baking powder, salt, nutmeg, cinnamon, sour cream and chopped nuts. Pour batter into 9x13" greased pan. Top with brown sugar, cinnamon and chopped nuts mix together. Cover, wrap and refrigerate overnight. Bake at 350° 40-45 min. Do not over bake.

Servings: 16
Preparation Time: 30 minutes
Start to finish: 24 hours

1 cup sugar
1/2 cup brown sugar
3/4 cup margarine
2 cups flour
1 teaspoon baking powder
1/2 teaspoon salt
1/2 teaspoon nutmeg
1/2 teaspoon cinnamon
1 cup sour cream
1 cup chopped nuts
1/2 cup brown sugar
1 teaspoon cinnamon
1/4 cup chopped nuts

Nutritional Values:
Per Serving (excluding unknown items): 316 Calories; 18g Fat (49.9% calories from fat); 4g Protein; 37g Carbohydrate; 2g Dietary Fiber; 6mg Cholesterol; 210mg Sodium.
Points: 7

Substitute Values:
Per Serving (using omit nuts, sugar substitutes, fat-free sour cream, and margarine): 242 Calories; 9g Fat (47.0% calories from fat); 3g Protein; 19g Carbohydrate; 1g Dietary Fiber; 2mg Cholesterol; 232mg Sodium.
Points: 5

U.S. to Metric Capacity

1/5 teaspoon = 1 ml
1 teaspoon = 5 ml
1 tablespoon = 15 ml
1 fluid oz. = 30 ml
1/5 cup = 50 ml
1 cup = 240 ml
2 cups (1 pint) = 470 ml
4 cups (1 quart) = .95 liter
4 quarts (1 gal.) = 3.8 liters

Weight
1 oz. = 28 grams
1 pound = 454 grams

Cooking Measurement Equivalents

16 tablespoons = 1 cup
12 tablespoons = 3/4 cup
10 tablespoons + 2 teaspoons = 2/3 cup
8 tablespoons = 1/2 cup
6 tablespoons = 3/8 cup
5 tablespoons + 1 teaspoon = 1/3 cup
4 tablespoons = 1/4 cup
2 tablespoons = 1/8 cup
2 tablespoons + 2 teaspoons = 1/6 cup
1 tablespoon = 1/16 cup
2 cups = 1 pint
2 pints = 1 quart
3 teaspoons = 1 tablespoon
48 teaspoons = 1 cup

Metric to U.S. Capacity

1 militers = 1/5 teaspoon
5 ml = 1 teaspoon
15 ml = 1 tablespoon
30 ml = 1 fluid oz.
100 ml = 3.4 fluid oz.
240 ml = 1 cup
1 liter = 34 fluid oz.
1 liter = 4.2 cups
1 liter = 2.1 pints
1 liter = 1.06 quarts
1 liter = .26 gallon

Weight
1 gram = .035 ounce
100 grams = 3.5 ounces
500 grams = 1.10 pounds
1 kilogram = 2.205 pounds
1 kilogram = 35 oz.

Half and half substitute recipe:
7/8 cup milk
7/8 tablespoon melted butter, cooled
combine and pour your desired measurement

INDEX

Made in the USA
Monee, IL
26 April 2023